OLDER MEMBERS
IN THE
CONGREGATION

OLDER MEMBERS
IN THE
CONGREGATION

by

Arthur P. Rismiller

AUGSBURG PUBLISHING HOUSE
Minneapolis   Minnesota

OLDER MEMBERS IN THE CONGREGATION

Foreword

The timeliness of such a book as this is underscored by the vastly increasing number of older people in our communities today. In well-established congregations the proportion of the aged is no longer negligible. They often represent as large a group as the teen-agers, for whom we are rightly prepared to make provision at some cost. A youth worker is often the first staff person, after the pastor, to be added to the pay roll. We recognize the crucial challenge of youth work because their future, and the future of the congregation, are at stake.

Yet the future of older members is every bit as crucial despite their shorter life-expectancy. Having arrived at that stage at which their final life-assignments are to be completed, some are not prepared, some need guidance, and all need strong support. They must be able to look to the congregation for help.

Few congregations are well enough informed or organized to offer that help. Perhaps it is because, at the rate of 1,000 reaching the age of 65 every day in our country, the sheer number of the aged has crept up on us and caught us napping. Hopefully, it is not because we have deliberately downgraded the significance of those who have comparatively few years to live!

Most of us covet an old age which is serene, cozy, and full of rich memories, present purpose, and future hope. Many have not prepared for such an old age and find themselves insecure, abandoned, bitter, and afraid when old age comes.

The Lord of the Church does not counsel us to let these unfortunates "stew in their own juice." He sends us to them, and to their happier contemporaries, with good news: the Gospel. Sermons and prayers, hymns and Sacraments are means of communicating that Gospel. They must have access to such opportunities. But the Gospel is ministered as often through the thoughtfulness, patience, understanding, and helpfulness to which Christ commits his people.

A congregation which will study this book in committee, and then proceed imaginatively and thoughtfully to institute its programs of service, will have made a good beginning in meeting the needs of its aged members and friends.

> G. S. THOMPSON, Executive Secretary
> Division of Welfare
> National Lutheran Council

Contents

Introduction 9

Some Facts About the Older Person 13

What Life Offers the Older Person 16

Changes Facing the Older Person 20

Basic Needs of the Older Person 28

If We Fail the Older Person 32

Working with the Older Person 39

The Church Can Help the Older Person 43

The Worship Life of the Older Person 47

Fellowship for the Older Person 66

Visitor's Service for the Older Person 97

Special Workers for the Older Person 115

Bibliography 123

Introduction

The purpose of this book is to provide a body of material which may be used by churches as a guide in their program of services to the older members of the congregation. That there should be guides of such nature is born of the volume of requests that have come from the many who are testing ways of broadening their outreach to their seniors. This request has been answered, in part, by guides which have been prepared to assist leaders of congregations. This guide, however, has been prepared as informative and directive material for both leaders and workers, but especially for lay workers.

That there should be emphasis upon concern for the older members in the congregation rests upon the development which has taken place among us, the growing number of older people. There have always been older people in the membership, but

9

never so many in comparison with those of other age groups in the congregation. Moreover, customary ways of our people and existing circumstances have made it difficult for older people to be included and to remain active in the life of the congregation. Thus there exists much opportunity for service, and it is the purpose of this book to assist the congregation in its services to the older members.

Before action, however, there must be understanding of older people as to their needs and what can occur when their needs are not met. There must be understanding so that older members can be helped in the way that they need to be helped and that they, in turn, may give their help so that the whole congregation can be effective in serving the community and the church at large.

It, therefore, is the purpose of this book to assist the members of the Christian congregation so that they can, according to ability and resources, help and befriend the older members in their various needs.

The Division of Welfare, National Lutheran Council, proposes the following charter for services to the aging:

Changing social patterns make it necessary for the church to review its charitable endeavors for the purpose of keeping these services consistent with the most enlightened developments of the day. The church must meet the needs of older people through congregational programs, through agencies and institutions, by supporting these services to the fullest of its abilities, as well as by alerting and stimulating community and government to assume their responsibilities to the aging.

It is the privilege of the older person

To be a witness for Christ in soundness of faith, love, and patience; sharing that which is good; exemplifying behavior as becomes a mature Christian.

To be active and alert in finding and cultivating friends; developing interests and skills; serving neighbors and community; adapting to new conditions and circumstances; recognizing his worth and usefulness as a redeemed child of God.

It is the responsibility of the church

To assure the older person of the opportunity to live in dignity as a child of God, redeemed by Christ; to worship God with full and complete access to the Means of Grace; to participate in regular and special activities as a member of the congregation.

To guide the family in its Christian duty of honoring the older person by encouraging maximum self-determination; assuring privacy of person and thoughts; fostering skill and abilities.

To stimulate the community to accept its share in the responsibility of providing for employment, based on ability; housing suited to the needs of older people; education and recreation, releasing potentials for growth; health care, dedicated to the preservation of human dignity; a basic income, assuring decent living standards.

The older members should be remembered, and rewarded, for they:

Have helped to plant our congregations.

Have helped to build our churches.

Have helped to make the church a living force in the community.

Have given more of themselves and their means in the work of the congregation than any other group, as we use the measure of years.

Have helped to spread the church's message across the seas and throughout the world.

For all this, most certainly, they should be helpfully remembered by their fellow members. This remembrance includes their continuance in the life and activity of the congregation. They do not wish to rest on past laurels but want to be useful to their congregation and their church where so much of their life has been given meaning.

Some Facts About

THE OLDER PERSON

When is a person old? There is no simple answer, as is illustrated by an interview with a patient in a geriatric hospital. "How old do you think I am?" said the patient. The chaplain replied, "Won't you tell me so I may know?" The patient responded this way: "People who see me say that I look to be fifty. Actually I am sixty-five, but you know, I really feel like ninety."

This is in keeping with the complicated facts about aging:

Some are old in body but young in mind.

Others are young in body but old in mind.

Physical capacities are usually at their peak in the twenties and then decline by various ratios in different persons.

Mental capacities, too, reach their peak in the late twenties or early thirties. But from that point on some persons have little perceptible decline while others show obvious impairment in their later years. Hence it is said of one that he is young for his years; of another that he is old for his years.

Commonly 65 is thought of as the age when the older years begin. Various agencies, places of business, and industries use this figure. Social Security, and other pension systems, usually pivot on the year 65; and so, generally, we enroll a person with the older ones when he has had 65 birthdays.

However, old age can be an attitude and not a matter of years. We may say a person is old when:

He finds little that is appealing to him.

He is not interested in seeing what is around the corner.

He looks back and does not want to look forward.

He hopes that the ringing telephone is not for him.

He waits for the sunset instead of looking for the sunrise.

Data About Older Persons

There are 18,000,000 in our country today who are 65 years of age or over. They represent nearly 10% of our population. Their number is steadily increasing. Since 1950 alone there has been an increase from 12,165,000 to the present number, which is more than 1,000 per day. Project estimates are of 24.5 million by 1980; 32.3 million by the turn of the century.

The average life span is now 70 years, a little more than that for women and a little less for men. The women outnumber the men.

Golden wedding anniversaries are celebrated by nearly half of all couples, whereas fifty years ago approximately 20% celebrated that event.

A strong majority of the women are widowed or single.

Only about 1½ million live on the farm, the others are urban dwellers.

They may have an adequate income but probably not. The social security system has become a foundation for financial support.

They would like to have more to do but the opportunities are meager. About 2 million are working full time. Nearly one-half need better living arrangements. About the same number live in homes that are more than 50 years old.

Data is almost endless, but the point is: This is an age of age! In our day age is not to be thought of as something unusual.

We all have a common interest in aging, and the congregation has a tremendous share in answering the question: "What will a man do with his years, especially when he is retired?"

What Life Offers

THE OLDER PERSON

He has traveled a path of many experiences which have contributed toward making him the individual older person that he is.

He has been active, going about his daily work, which he accepted by choice or by dint of circumstances, and by it he made his way in life—creatively and economically.

He probably wished at times that he could have left his work for a day or two, with its problems and headaches, and "gone fishing" or seen how the rest of the world lived. It didn't work out that way, for the job he held down also held him down.

He noted from time to time that life was moving along. He still felt much the same; but in his appearance changes were taking place—he was getting older, wrinkled and stooped.

He began losing some of his physical drive; but he could counterbalance this with more wisdom, gained by experience, and so he continued to be an efficient person.

He began thinking about the later years.

Then came the day of retirement. Due recognition was accorded him for his long and faithful service.

He probably felt at the time that his retirement was a great thing. He could do what he wanted to do, at his own pace, and go where he wanted to go at a time of his own choosing. He could do things at his own leisure.

What things? He soon found the list of them to be short, and then even shorter, with dwindling opportunities to multiply them. And then time began to hang heavily on his hands.

He really discovered for the first time, in all its fulness, that retirement was a change, almost a shock. It was like starting all over again.

He noted that he could not purchase things as he used to. His income was drastically different. He had to use extreme caution. His pension was not reaching nearly as far as he had thought it would. He felt financial insecurity. He became somewhat anxious. Would his money hold out? Would it meet developing needs? Would he become dependent on others? On his children? On society?

Financial uncertainty impressed him with the need of being austerely saving. Maybe, unknowingly, he became a hoarder in his attempt to establish security feelings, the hoarded items or funds serving as symbols of position and strength.

Sometimes he felt quite secure because he had such inner resources as his trust in God, his faith in men and belief in himself; but sometimes he felt quite insecure, lost-like, as though life was passing by and he had little part in it.

He noted changes in himself. He couldn't remember as he once did. Names and dates kept slipping away from him, and since he had fewer things to occupy his mind and hands, he spent more time thinking about himself. His aches and pains seemed to have increased. Likely they had been there before, but now he dwelt on them.

He had been so busy in his productive years that he had taken no time to develop a hobby. Thus he now had less opportunity to express the feelings and tastes of his personality.

He looked up old friends and realized, perhaps fully for the first time, how many of them had moved or slipped away.

He experienced, sooner or later, the loss of spouse. The house was empty, a loved voice no longer was heard, and intimate matters weren't shared as before.

Actually, the older person comes to the place where he can decide whether he will give up, be through with productive life, or whether he will accept the time he now has at his disposal to build new interests and seek new social relationships. But this is a severe test. If he waits for life to come to him, it won't. If he goes out to find it, he can. How-

ever, he needs encouragement, sometimes guidance. He does not want sympathy, but understanding.

The congregation can supply much of this. It is a group of people who have been born of God and as such they have concern for people—any people— hence for the older members.

Changes Facing

THE OLDER PERSON

It has been pointed out that the older person comes to the place where he must face up to changes, that in a sense it is like "starting all over again." He has to make adjustments. If he does not do so he may contribute to the deterioration of his personality. But when he tries to do so he is apt to face frustrations. There are barriers and pitfalls in his way, and a number of these are there because they have been placed before him by our society.

A. *Where Will He Live?*

Alone? The older person frequently comes to this, by choice or by circumstances; but many suffer from lack of companionship.

With someone? This often is not satisfying because the housemate is not a compatible person.

With children? The older person, unless he is a dependent person, really does not want to do this. He respects the right of his children to the privacy of their own family. He feels that he may be intruding or that he may not be free to plan for himself. He may have fears about surrendering his own independence.

In a home for the aging? The older person frequently expresses fears about such an arrangement. He has impressions about institutional life. Some of it is less than appealing to him, for it seems to him that his own personality will simply be swallowed up in an institution.

If at all possible the older person should live where he wants to live. Happiest living is when he can live as he has lived—where he has made his home. Often our own fears about his ability to do this are projected on him to his discomfort. We will do best to have the older person live where he wants to live until he voluntarily expresses fear about his ability to do so.

B. *Society Places Emphasis on the Young*

In education—for schools have been geared to children and youth. Opportunities for adult education have, in large measure, been out of reach for the older person.

In complex problems—the older person finds that there is a field of trained people to guide and aid the young. But what about help for himself in his problems and complex situations?

In employment—the older person discovers that youth is favored at the employment window. Mass production and an impersonal industrial economy lay the hand of choice on youth and speed.

There is developing a core of belief, however, that more is needed than youth and speed—like competence, experience, reliability, and mature wisdom. This is a goal and there is movement in this direction; but in the main, the older person still finds that the ring and the crown are put on the finger and the head of youth.

Emphasis should be placed on the young.

Emphasis should be placed on every age.

Emphasis, in equal proportion, needs to be seen and felt by the older members in our congregations.

The church can be an advocate and crusader to this end: for the church believes in the worth of every man at every age.

C. *A Shift in Values*

Frequently the older person finds that values have changed:

From experience to knowledge.
From quality to quantity.
From safety to speed.
From participation to observation.
From practitioner to expert.

D. *False Opinions About Older People*

That they want to be left alone, to live on their memories. But this isn't so. They want to be interested in people, ideas, and things and to experience the interest of others in them and in their ideas.

That they are different from others because they are old. But it isn't so. Each person faces a different set of circumstances, but all have the same basic feelings.

That they want to be cozy and safe. But it isn't so. They want to do and to dare. There are older persons who want to be waited on, and fussed over, just as there are children or grown people who, in their dependency, want to be waited on. Some use childhood patterns to fall back on when stamina, will power, and emotions have broken down, and so they remain children in their adult years.

That they fit the saying that "An old dog cannot be taught new tricks." But it isn't so. Older persons can know and do new things. They just do so at a slower rate than when they were young.

That they are grouchy. But it isn't so. It is no more so than with persons of any other age. They may have more reasons to be grouchy, but they are not that way unless they have always been that way.

We see, then, that the older person has to deal with frustrations in his attempt to adjust to the changes with which he is confronted. Sometimes these are self-imposed, but mostly they are due to practices in our society.

Our modern world has indeed produced many and varied benefits for mankind: better living standards, better housing for people, better health conditions, opportunities for broader communication among all people. But with these benefits the modern world has also produced many stresses and strains for the older people. Our communities have become quite rigid in channeling older people into imposed modes of living—without the conscious cooperation of the older people themselves.

The stark facts about our culture with reference to older people is that, in practice, they are frequently rejected, doors are frequently closed to them, and sometimes hostility toward them is expressed.

In this climate there is need for better understanding of older people, of their feelings and problems. It may be assumed that church people are most sensitive to the painful feelings of men. Therefore:

The church should be alert to the pains of aging.

The church should show its concern by word and deed.

The church should educate for maturity.

The church should be positive in its attitudes toward older members in the congregation and give a demonstration of how older people are not rejected but accepted. Indeed, *our congregations can take the lead in making a new age for old age.*

E. *The Changing Status of Older Persons in a Changing Society*

A representative American today is an urban dweller. This is a change. When the older person of our day was a child, the representative American lived and worked in a rural setting. This change has come about rather swiftly. In the span of two generations we have changed from a rural to an urban society. Before the majority lived and made their living on the farm or from it; now only a small segment of our people—roughly ten percent—make their living that way, the remainder living or working in a highly complex, industrial community.

This has caused personal status changes.

Before, the representative American:

Lived on a farm.

Worked for himself, usually on the farm which he owned.

Had a large family with growing children sharing in the farm work who, upon their marriage, settled in the community and remained in a close family relationship.

Supervised his own work and adjusted his daily schedule to conform to his will

Lived in a close-knit rural neighborhood of common interests and vocations.

Was the breadwinner for the family.

Retired by choice, usually by degree, based on physical capability.

Continued to live on the economic means provided by the farm.

Filled his days by following the seasonal farm work.

Felt needed as he was sought out on the basis of his knowledge and experience.

Now, the representative American:

Lives in the city.

Works for someone else, frequently in relationship to a complex office, corporation, industrial setting.

Has a smaller family with growing children unrelated to his vocation who, upon their marriage, become scattered as a part of a highly mobile society.

Being supervised in his work, is subject to a schedule to which he conforms.

Lives in an urban community where many, because of the variety of patterns of daily living, go their different ways.

Is one of several in the family who is employed.

Retires by directive, usually at the age of 65.

Is dependent on pension funds, often inadequate for his needs.

Finds, in his retirement, that it is often difficult to occupy the time of the passing days.

Has to deal with feelings of being unneeded as he is separated from former work and activity roles.

(The bulletin supplement to "Adding Life to Years," No. 4, Volume VI, published by the Institute of Gerentology, State University of Iowa, carries a report to the governor of the State of Iowa. It includes a listing from the Council of State Governments of the Typical Rural Neighborhood of Seventy Years Ago and the Typical Urban Community of the Present. The listing serves well to project the Representative American.)

The basic effect of these changes has been to decrease the activities and the social contacts of the developing person, for the aging person is still a developing one. The changing patterns tend to cast the older individual into a passive role. This is a role that is unnatural.

Anyone, except in abnormal circumstances, desires involvement with life in its everyday aspects. He does not want to see it pass before his eyes but wants to be a part of it. The older person, though, is too often left out.

We have not fully applied ourselves to bettering his lot; we have been slow to integrate man, in his later years, into social involvement.

This situation poses a challenge for the church. The task is to meet man at his place of need. The message of the church is helpful: of an unchanging God in a changing age, of a God who blesses every change that is good. In our congregations planning and action will follow concern for the older members, for each is important in the household of God.

Basic Needs of

THE OLDER PERSON

The needs of older persons are several and of several sorts; some are peculiar to the aged, some are quite common to mankind. The surprising fact is that the basic needs of the elderly are the same as those of all persons regardless of age. These may be defined as:

SECURITY—peace with God, a continuing support of their spiritual hunger, emotional balance, a place to call their own, funds enough to be self-sustaining or, using the words of Luther, "food and clothing, home and family."

RECOGNITION—to be accepted as persons, accepted for what they are and not for what they once were, for they have an abhorrence of being put on the shelf and being made observers of life instead of participators.

BELONGING—being loved and being able to love another in turn. The far-away look of many an older person conveys the pining to belong to someone.

NEW EXPERIENCES—to exercise the faculties of body, mind, and soul. To live in the current of today instead of lingering in the shadow of yesterday. To be useful and to have a purpose, for the lack of purpose is a form of death, and inaction means stagnation. God has a vineyard and a marketplace, but too often older people can't get in because of human barriers.

ILLUSTRATIVE CASE HISTORIES

Security—B. K. is 83 years of age and lives in his apartment all alone. He lost his wife some years ago. He lives on Social Security—67 dollars per month. There isn't enough to live on. He has outlived his friends, and no one comes to see him any more. He lives in constant and terrible insecurity. How do I know? Because he tells me about the people who come to his window to watch him and about the people in the tree at his living room window telling him that they are soon going to take over his apartment. He tells me about the people who lie in his bed, so he can't get in and have his sleep. No, these people are not real, but nevertheless they are real to him. When he tells me about all this, it's as if he were saying, "I feel so terribly insecure."

Recognition—Mr. R. used to be an officer in his congregation. He has been a widower for a number of years and has no children. He now lives in a home for older people. Of ailments he has but one: he is sick in heart. When I call on him he starts the conversation and carries it on from there. He talks and he talks. All I need to do is to listen. He goes from one thing to another. The only response he asks of me is that I indicate agreement with him on a point that he is making. You see, his talking is just a symptom. What it all means is that he wants to be recognized. He wants to monopolize my attention so he can satisfy his feeling of wanting to be recognized as someone worth while.

Belonging—Mrs. T. is 70 and is living in a home for the aged. Sometimes she is well and sometimes she is sick. When she is sick she is taken to the infirmary and after several weeks usually recuperates to the point that she can take care of herself in her dormitory room. It is then that her need is so nakedly seen, her need to belong. She will sit for hours, all by herself, in a shady spot out on the lawn. Usually, when we talk with her, she speaks about her family. But there is just one daughter left, living quite some distance away. Mrs. T. will tell of her close association with her family and one gets the impression of her sense of belonging, which she now misses. She has not yet allowed herself to form new associations. When a group is gathered together Mrs. T. will stand at the door and look in, longingly. When she comes to chapel she will sit in a corner or at the fringe of the group. She looks longingly, at times, from one to the other. When you shake her hand she holds on, releasing it grudgingly. She wants to be a part of the group, to participate, to belong. She is unhappy and the task is to help her to find closeness with others, like the closeness she had with her family.

New Experiences—Virginia, who demonstrates this need so well, was never married. She is not a skilled person. For years she made her living by working in a factory. But this is all behind her now. She is going on 60 and was never able to secure employment after she was laid off about ten years ago. This was after a period of hospitalization and convalescence—when she was told that her services would no longer be required. She wants to work. She would do anything if she could just get a job of some kind; but you see, you don't get jobs, when unskilled, after 40 or 50, sometimes not even when skilled. So do you know what she does? She sits in her room and works with needle and thread and yarn. She has no special talent in this direction but she makes some ill formed contrivance and gives it to me. What she gives to me is like a voice which says, "I can work! I can do something! I am showing you that I can be active and can do something which is worth while." It's like a haunting voice. What she needs is to have some new experiences, meaningful to her and others.

Security, recognition, belonging, new experiences—these are the needs of the older members in the congregation in which the congregation becomes involved as it practices the principles which are based on the Gospel of Jesus Christ.

If We Fail

THE OLDER PERSON

The needs which we have pointed out are basic to the well-being of every person. When these needs are not met in the older person, or when the individual has given up in his effort to satisfy them, he uses various defense mechanisms to protect himself.

As far back as 1948, M. Gittelson, writing in *Geriatrics* 3:135 on "The Emotional Problems of Elderly People," saw some developing patterns of adjustment to old age. He cited:

A decreased memory for recent events.

A sharpening of memory for the past.

A self-assertive attitude to overcome insecurity.

A mild depression caused by isolation and loneliness.

Introversion and increased sensitivity.

A free-floating anxiety caused by the death of those of the same age group, especially when relatives are involved.

Here was the beginning in an orientation to patterns of living observed in older people as they found difficulty in adjusting to a new world of old age.

Since that time many studies have been made, observations classified, and clinics conducted to further a broader understanding of the involvements that are associated with the lengthening span of life. It is important that it be so for such investigations have made clear that our understanding and concern are a part, and vitally so, in assisting seniors to fulfill their real needs. Here is where the congregation can function in a valuable way, through its parish programs, to assist older people in their adjustments to the problems of life. Such basic needs as to be loved, to belong and to be useful can be found in the church.

When needs are not met, defenses are utilized, sometimes in a conscious way, but more often unconsciously, to protect the self. When basic needs are not met, defenses like the following can be observed:

WITHDRAWAL. Instead of meeting life at the points of its opportunities and enjoying the offered challenges, there is instead a shrinking from it all. As the older person becomes less flexible and rigid in his ability to adapt, he feels threatened as he is confronted with the issues and problems rising before him. In an effort to guard and to secure existing identity, stimuli are circumvented, through withdrawal, so that adjustments need not be made to what seems unsafe or upsetting. Instead of coming to grips with the problems and the active forces confronting him in his daily environment, the older person, feeling his reserves depleted, simply withdraws to avoid the issues. It is interesting to note that failing sight and hearing are sometimes used as excuses to avoid contact with environmental stimulation. We have heard it said that someone "sees, but does not see." The situation is applicable to older people, for some see only what they want to see, and hear but do not hear. This is a type of withdrawal, for by this method the diversity of confusing things is eliminated. The implication is that it is painful and disturbing to get close to realities as they are and that it would be far more pleasant just to deny what is seen and heard. All people do this, of course, in some degree, but such a defense system is often noted among seniors as they suffer unfulfilled needs. By simply withdrawing there is escape from further problems.

TURNING TO THE PAST. To find satisfaction, when it is denied in the present, there is a turning to the events in the past which were meaningful and satisfying. The past offers a refuge where experiences, which were good, can be relived. We are all familiar with older people who tell, and retell, of the times when they were recognized. In time, however, this becomes dissatisfying and the older person turns even more to the past and depends on the pleasant memories of youth and childhood to sustain him. The ultimate is that some even regress to the level of infancy, with incontinence and utter dependency.

COMPENSATION. The older person, impressed with feelings of waning capacities, is motivated to do something about it. Restricted as to resources, he may do some avid reading, cramming himself with information, ideas, and facts, to balance felt losses in other areas. He may slavishly apply himself to master some new field. Healthy developments can come from an effort at compensation, but when the effort is made for the sake of proving self-worth, it is symptomatic of the lack of ease.

For example: a skilled watchmaker holds his watch in his hands and deftly and surely applies his necessary tools; as he gets older and finds it difficult to apply his tools because of unsteady hands he braces his arms, or hands, to assist him to steadiness—a good example of compensation. However, when we discover the person who has retired, or has dropped from gainful employment because of waning capabilities, embarking upon some slavish application to a new venture, going on in an attempt to impress others with his knowledge and know-how, we become aware of the lurking insecurity behind it all. An extension of this method produces the pseudopodiac (existing on a false base), not rare, who dearly holds on to familiar ideas or items, making them apparent to all, to bolster his inner security. The "hold-on" is important. Thus he may wish to hold on to his socks, in bed or out, or to take his money with him when he goes to the bathroom. What he really needs, of course, is not to prove his capabilities but to feel accepted, just as he is, by others.

DEPRESSION. Frequently the older person, confronted with losses related to meaningful living, lapses into depression. He means well, tries again—harder and harder, but finds repetition of denials and lapses into depression. It is not uncommon to see among older people those who feel they are burdened down with denials and frustrations. It's like eating the crumbs of life when once life's full meal was the fare. Some take refuge in depression, defending themselves in this manner. Conversation with them reveals that they feel cut off from the full stream of living. They present a picture of lonely persons. It is as if they are overwhelmed by these feelings, and utter it with a long sigh. The lapsing is like saying, "I feel cut off from life. It is all around me but I am not a part of it."

The congregation can be helpful to such a person both in prevention and in healing. Indeed, the members may be so caught up in the rush of affairs that they fail to sense the feeling of those whose lives they touch but briefly. That is part of the trouble. The admonition of the Lord is that members be there for the next man in his need. Here is one in need. And Christian fellowship is exactly what is required to prevent his use of lapsing into depression as a defense against loss of meaningful relationships in affairs and with persons.

SELF-CENTEREDNESS. When outgoing interests cannot be centered in activity and in other persons, then they are readily centered in self. The person's interests are turned inward and he puts himself under increased observation. Shortcomings are magnified. Pains grow out of proportion. Organs of the body are considered to be functioning improperly. Self-interest holds the center of the stage of life. Unconcerned about life around him, the person becomes very dissatisfied and, to protect himself, places the blame for his predicament on others. It would be unreasonable to blame himself, so he blames others. The end result is that he becomes a bitter person and his personality disintegrates. A congregation of concerned people, concerned about an individual, is a help which negates the felt need on the part of that individual to protect himself by resorting to self-centeredness.

GENERAL ANXIETY. The older person comes to the place in life where he is faced with an increasing number of reversals. Loss of independence, loss of income, loss of friends, loss of spouse, loss of strength or health are experienced. It means that the older person is constantly called on for self-testing. Repeatedly he confronts himself, consciously or unconsciously, with the question: Can I do it? Am I able? Am I still worth while? Do I measure up? The need of self-testing creates an atmosphere of uncertainty and some, not fully able to handle their reversals succumb to anxiety. This anxiety may be consciously felt, and expressed day after day, making the person miserable and ill. Or it may be unconsciously felt, causing the person to resort to depression, dissociation from others, or to stubborn patterns of living. A necessary medicine for such a person is concern from others, a concern which the congregation is able to demonstrate.

Working with

THE OLDER PERSON

In our concern for older persons and in our desire to work with them, we can make common mistakes. It is good to list them and make a study of them, for they will be seen as ways which actually bypass the feelings and desires of older persons, forcing them to withdraw instead of encouraging them to seek outlets for their personality and inner drives.

THE WORKER WILL AVOID

Planning for Older Persons

There is a variety of adverse experiences which are related to the senior years. Retirement, loss of income, loss of spouse, lack of vocational challenge, health problems—all of these raise the possibility of serious problems for the elderly. There can be considerable confusion intertwined, or shock can immobilize the individual. The helper's temptation then

is to plan for the elders and to point out the course
they should take. The danger in this is that we take
away the desire of the person to help himself or to
imply that he can lean on someone else. This de-
stroys inner strength. In planning we will want to
plan with, not for, the older person so that by his
own decisions he can maintain his convictions that
he can still meet life. When such planning is with,
and through, the Holy Spirit, our older persons keep
growing.

Emphasizing Old Age

This means subscription to the notion that "after
all you are old, so what can you expect?" As a matter
of fact years have little to do with the feelings of
an individual. At any age we can love, respond, appreciate, plan, hope, and so on. We will find that
we can be far more constructive when we forget
that a person is "old" and deal with him as a personality. He is a personality who can meet with us
on the common ground of human feelings and re-
sponses. If a man is not penalized by years, he should
not be penalized by attitudes.

Making Life Too Easy for Him

The average older person wants to make his own
way. He wants to do something with the life he has.
He does not want to sit and wait, yearn with empti-

ness, rust, and slowly die. It is unfair to him to approach him with the advice, "You have always worked hard and now we want you to take a rest"; or, "Here is a nice shawl to put around your shoulders while you rest in your rocking chair"; or, "You save your strength and we will do it for you." Our older persons want to take their place with the rest of us, to "live" with us. We do them injustice when, by fact or inference, we shunt them from the core of human activity. In fact, to do so is to contribute to feelings of self-depreciation on their part.

THINKING OF OLD AGE AS CLOSING SCENE OF LIFE

Life is often spoken of as a book with chapters: a chapter on childhood, one on youth, one on maturity, and the final one on old age. This does not fit in with the Christian view of life. True life does not run out like the sands in an hour glass but it goes on and on, with differing scenes in time which eventually merge in the great scene of "world without end." Life is always the same gift from God though experienced from different points of vantage. Old age, then, is not an end, but a new frame in which to approach all the challenges and opportunities which are so wonderfully given.

The church, with her knowledge of God and her view of eternity, is most capable of giving our older people the long view of life—the continuing view of life—in the place of one that has different periods, or chapters, and ends with old age. The church, in love, extends this concept of life to its people of all ages. The congregation is where this concept is put into practice.

The Church Can Help

THE OLDER PERSON

1. By strengthening the spiritual ministry among the aging, supplying the ingredients of spiritual and emotional security.

2. By reaching out to the aging in the congregation, and the community with a program of visitation, entering the lives of these older adults with a demonstration of Christian concern and personal interest. Such a program can fulfill a basic need of those whose circle of intimates has grown small.

3. By providing facilities and leadership to further social opportunities among the older members like Golden Age Clubs, providing in such settings the fellowship which is so basic to life.

4. By strengthening all services of Christian concern within the congregation to make it possible for the older members to remain in their own homes as

long as it is possible to do so. This serves the double purpose of leaving the aging in the surroundings where they are at home and of slackening the ever growing lists of those who are finding it necessary to make applications for sheltered care.

5. By utilizing the talents of the older members in the many facets of congregational life, affording them the privilege of interesting and constructive experiences. Without such opportunity life becomes empty and being empty, disintegrates.

While it cannot be assumed that such strategy will solve all the problems related to the aging members within the congregation, it can be said that such activity supplies the framework essential to the well-being of the aging individuals: Security, Recognition, Fellowship and Meaningful Experiences. The older people confront the congregation! They do not ask to be made over, nor do they want to be left alone. They do ask to be included in the on-going stream of life.

COMMITTEE ON THE AGING

The usual medium of study for any contemplated action by a congregation is a committee. Within the framework of the congregation there needs to be a committee, of some kind, which concerns itself with services to different groups within the membership. With the growing volume of older people there needs to be a committee, on a continuing basis, which concerns itself with the services the congregation can render these seniors. Like the children, the youth, the young people and the adults, so the older members need to be included in a congregation's study of how best it can serve its people.

A committee will:

Include representation from older people.

Conduct a survey to get a true, informative, picture about the older members. (Another can be made relative to the entire community. A guide, for survey purposes follows.)

Study all data closely.

Make recommendations of programs and services.

Give assistance in putting plans into action.

PERIODIC SURVEYS

From time to time surveys can be made which will provide up-to-date information about older members.

A sample form follows:

Name of church................. Location...........
Type: City......... Town......... Country.........
  Year of establishment...............................
Membership number.........Number over 65.........
  Number of men......... Number of women.........
How many, over 65, attend church services?............
How many, over 65, attend Sunday school?............

How many, over 65, are in organizations? . . . .

How many, over 65, are leaders-officers? . . . .

How many, over 65, are on committees? . . . .

How many, over 65, are serving in a volunteer
   capacity in congregational activities? . . . .

How many live alone? . . . . Married couples? . . . .

   With children? . . . . With relatives? . . . .

How many are widows? . . . . Widowers? . . . .

How many older members are shut-in? . . . .

   Does the congregation have any regular
      program for visitation? . . . .

How many older members are home-bound? . . . .

   Does the congregation have any regular
      program to provide transportation?

How many older members are in rest homes? . . . .

   Is there a regular program to keep
      in touch with them? . . . .

Are any seniors in financial straits? . . . .

   Are community resources applied? . . . .

Are there older people who are inactive, having
   little or nothing to do? . . . .

   Does the congregation provide older people
      with activity opportunities? . . . .

Are unchurched, inactive, elderly sought out? . . . .

The Worship Life of

THE OLDER PERSON

The writer, working among older people, frequently hears someone say, "I used to belong to church." Or, "No one from my church has called on me for a long time." It is true that a considerable number, who might be active, do not feel that they are among the "belonging."

Involved in the situation are two possibilities:

The older person himself may be at fault. In his effort to adjust himself to the role of an older person he may find the effort outweighing the satisfactions, leading him to take refuge in withdrawal and inactivity, projecting criticism of himself upon his church or just giving way to a feeling of uselessness.

On the other hand, it is possible for a congregation to be unmindful of the needs and feelings of the older member and allow him to slip out of the fellowship of the congregation. The members of the church will do well to remember that the older person is traveling some untried paths and, in his increasing dependency, needs encouragement and assistance.

If the congregation will anticipate the needs of its older members, effort can be made to forestall the occurrence of deep problems in their lives.

The thing to do is to keep the older members in the worship and life of the church as fully as possible and as long as possible.

There is a double approach:

Integrate them with all ages in all programs.

Give them opportunity to group in their own age climate, out of consideration for their common interests. Even when the second approach is made, it is of utmost importance that they be kept integrated in the program of the congregation. They must not be segregated but integrated.

The pastor, the Sunday school, the organizations, and the worshiping congregation all have a part in integrating the seniors in the congregational program.

THE PART OF THE PASTOR

The pastor ought to be the hub of the congregation's concern. This does not mean, however, that he must carry all the responsibility. His is the prior responsibility, but a part of it is to delegate this work to the members of the congregation.

The pastor will study his own attitudes toward aging. Does he identify himself, perhaps unknowingly, more closely with those of his own age? Has he thought about his own aging?

The pastor will acquaint himself with the literature in the field of progressive work with the aging and with the resources in his community which are available to older people in his congregation.

The pastor will acquaint himself with the dynamics of aging: physical, psychological, social, and spiritual. This acquaintance will help him to be more effective in his application of the Gospel to the personal welfare of the older members.

The pastor will want to ponder how he may use all the educative processes of the congregation—confirmation class, Sunday school, study groups—to teach awareness of the need to prepare for the senior years.

The pastor will be called on to be a counselor to his older members. Counsel will be sought from him, but there will also be times when he will see a need while the older person does not. He can enter this role through his kindly interest. He will have to remember, however, that this role will be one that is time-consuming, for he will have to pace himself to the slower gait of the older person.

THE PART OF THE CONGREGATION

The congregation will always be mindful of its older members and give them equal opportunity, with all others, to serve and to be served. Most older people want to be completely a part of the total church program. Some desire segregation, but there is reason to believe that this is more a personality trait, or a compliance with custom, than a desire common to older people. There need be no question as to whether older members want to sit on the sidelines or whether they wish to do as they have always done in giving time, talent, and service. They are ready to go as far as their abilities allow. Be mindful of them.

The congregation's program needs to be based on the conviction that every individual has significance in the sight of God, regardless of age. This means that the congregation operates on the basis that every Christian has a growing edge and room for continuing development.

The congregation will have representatives from among the seniors on the planning boards and committees.

The congregation will undertake ways to keep the older members in the worship life of the church. Worship is vital; it leads to deepening and sustaining faith. The congregation should be alert to the older people's needs so that they do not, for any reasons which can be overcome—like lack of transportation, or lack of financial ability—drop out of the regular meetings for worship

The congregation must provide fellowship experiences for the older members so as to overcome loss of family and friends and to fortify them against feelings of self-depreciation.

The congregation serves the interest of senior members by giving them something to do for their church. Give them the opportunity.

The congregation will profit, as will the older members, when recognition is given them for services which they have performed in serving their Lord and his church.

The congregation must be therapeutic in its work, by practicing *tender, loving concern.*

This is caring—a personal caring which grows out of God's love. It is caring enough to:

Include the older members.
Assure them of being needed.
Create the feeling of being wanted.
Motivate them to participation.
Provide an environment which leads the older members to feel that they are wanted in the worship and life of the church.

This is not coddling them! It is not overindulging them! It is including them—as everybody else is included.

The congregation must minister positively to persons at their level of need. It cannot, by practice, add to the negative attitude often encountered that the older years are a sentence to be served rather than a blessing to be enjoyed.

WORKING WITH OLDER MEMBERS
WHO HAVE PROBLEMS

1. The older person needs someone to whom he can talk. In a sense his situation is like that of any other older person with unresolved problems, but in another sense it is his alone. He must be helped to put his problems into words. Many patterns adopted by seniors center in withdrawal, and they withdraw to such an extent that they fail to share their feelings with others. There is frequent expression of this fact in words like, "What's the use to say anything about it?" It's as if the person were saying, "No one will listen anyway." There is use. As the older person is helped to talk about his problem he begins to see it in clearer light. He needs someone to talk to, but he also needs someone who will take the time to listen. Pastor and people can be well intentioned, but it takes more, for the older person gives his trust fully only when he discovers that someone is really ready to give his time to listen. Often others, because of their role in life, cannot or do not provide the opportunity for the older person to tell them of their situation. Pastor, and people, help the older person with unresolved problems when they take the time to listen when he wants to talk.

2. The older person needs someone who, listening to his talk, will be aware of implied deeper meanings in concerning relationship. This means that the pastor, worker, or church member goes beyond the ac-

ceptance at face value of everything the older person says. He looks at the mood, feelings, and circumstances out of which the words are spoken. These have a language of their own which, together with the spoken word, reveal to the listener areas of concern on the part of the elderly individual. Thus, to look for that which is behind the words is important. For example:

When the older person speaks repeatedly about the times in his life when he was successful, he is really saying that he is turning away from the circumstances in which he now finds himself.

A complaint about food may be an indication that he feels unaccepted by those upon whom he is dependent.

Expressions about feelings of personal worthlessness may be allied to guilt feelings or to meager human relationships.

Constant, recurring complaints about ills and pains of the body suggest the possibility of dependency problems.

Expressions, or moods, indicating depression suggest that anger, aroused by current experiences, is being directed at his own person.

Implied, or spoken, suggestions that others slight him, or "have it in for him," often indicate that anger over frustrations, known or unrecognized, is turned on others.

Such examples are cited to alert the caller, or worker, to the need of understanding what the older person is really saying. Thus the worker is able to meet the older person at the level of difficulty, and to give him the feeling that he is really understood. Prescriptions like "cheer up" and "everything will work out all right" only cover up the difficulties which, unresolved, will rise again.

3. The older person needs a continuing, or sustained, relationship with someone, like his pastor or fellow church member, whom he has found to be a willing listener and who has shown understanding. Such a relationship serves to stimulate the older person to the conviction that he is recognized, accepted, appreciated, and that therefore he must be worth while after all. This assurance opens the door to hope and aids the older person to feelings of security. He then sees more of life as a whole and not just his part of present trials, difficulties, and even helplessness. His confidence is stabilized when he is aware that an understanding pastor or fellow member believes in him and he in turn is helped to believe in himself.

4. The older person needs to come to grips with the reality that difficulties are encountered at all age levels of life. He can be assisted to recognize this by talking about his trials and problems with an understanding, concerned person. The pastor, or member, in such a role, can help the older person to evaluate his attitude toward his individual circumstances. It is important that he realize that burdens are a part

of every period in life, even though there are some that are peculiar to the older years. The way in which he has met, and overcome, difficulties in past years can contribute significantly to feelings of capability in meeting current concerns. It is also important for the older person to realize that some problems can be resolved while others cannot, so that the former are resolved and the latter accepted and used creatively. Wholesome attitudes can, and do, grow out of heart-to-heart talks between the burdened person and his understanding companions.

5. The older person needs to be reassured that, though many changes have come to him, God has not changed. It is change which so often distresses the older person, giving rise to feelings of insecurity and anxiety. His role in life has changed; his circumstances have changed; his relationships have changed; and so he yearns for the world to "stay put" instead of confronting him with more change.

It is a heartening thing for a pastor and congregation to see the example of an older person, tried, but staunch in the faith and well possessed in his Christian life. Besides these there are also those who, because of stress, have times of wavering and uncertainty. It is not infrequent to find an older person expressing himself in terms of anxiety at the constant pressure to adjust to change. He experiences losses, due to aging, which intensify the anxiety. His losses can induce the feeling that he is useless, and sometimes, in that feeling, he has the impression that others, yes even God, considers him to be useless. We hear expressions like, "God has forgotten me," or, "God seems so far away."

Reassurance sustains, and none more so than reassurance of God's understanding and love. Such reassurance is made expressive to older people through the concerns shown them by members and workers of the congregation.

This does not mean, however, that all older people respond to spiritual comforting just because they are older. There is charted evidence that religious faith does not increase just because people become older. To those who know their Lord and have been in church life, however, reassurance of God's love is sustaining and for this reason necessary. In view of this, pastor and congregation will not only be aware of the need to win souls to Christ in the early years, but also be ready to give special attention to the reassurance of older people within the framework of the Gospel of love and life.

VISITING OLDER MEMBERS WHO ARE ILL

Illness is a broad term. It includes organic, mental, and emotional elements. It must never be forgotten that the older person, like any person, is a total person and not one who is compartmentalized into body, mind, and spirit. When the body is ill, the mind is going to have some attitudes about it; and when the mind must cope with unresolved problems and insufferable situations, the organs of the body are going to react to the tension. A vast battleground is the emotions—how the person feels about his experiences. Thus, what affects one area of life also affects all areas of life. Illness, therefore, may be a reaction to a distressing situation the older person is undergoing.

Why Do We Visit?

It is a responsibility. The older person who is ill has needs, in degree and in number, and these can cause him to feel that he is on an island, alone, separated from normal relations with mankind. These needs dictate that pastor and people of the congregation show their concern. It behooves them to communicate to the ill older members that:

The visitor, as a person, cares for him.

The people of the congregation, as evidenced in the person of the visitor, care for him.

God cares for him.

All the services of the pastor and the members of the congregation are meant to convey to the individual the assurance that God cares for him. This is what we want to communicate to the older member who is experiencing illness—whether the illness is physical in nature, whether the frame of mind indicates that he is seeking perspective in his current set of problems, or whether his emotional demonstrations indicate that there is internal conflict.

A warm interest in, and a concern for, our older member is a real requisite in the visiting ministry offered him. When we visit the ill we want to show our interest in the person we visit. To this end the circumstances of the surroundings, or the nature of the illness, must not deter us from the purpose of our visit—to indicate to the person that we care for him. And our service is given, not because of duty, but because we care for the person.

Whom Do We Visit?

The person who is reaching the place in his life where he is going to be included among those known as older persons. Such a time in life will not be without attendant changes—the unnatural situation of being unemployed, the relinquishing of professional activity, the curtailment of income, the physical handicaps associated with aging, and psychological changes. The helpful pastor and fellow church member can assist the person approaching the later years to face the changing prospects realistically. The implication of course is that to face changing prospects realistically is to ward off illness.

The person who has reached the retirement years. This is the time that adjustments are not a matter of prospect but a matter of the moment. The pastor and congregation can be watchful of the older member's success in adapting himself to retirement challenges. The aging person can be assisted in his recognition that the older years are still years for growth. Physical growth stops, or is erratic, but there is always room for spiritual growth, and mentally there is room for retention. Such growth tends to fend off illness.

The person who has reached the older years and is having difficulty in regulating his life to existing circumstances. The congregation of pastor and people can be watchful, at this time, for such symptoms as anxiety, mental lapses, depression, assertiveness, projection, regression, and the like. Such signs of changing personality will indicate that the older member may need some assistance in seeing his place in life in clearer light, changing what can be changed and accepting that which cannot be changed. Of significant help will be the spiritual resources which are held in common by the visitor and the one visited.

The person who has reached the older years and has succumbed to the forces which have eroded his self-respect and have caused him to be dependent on others. It is the time when the congregation will give the older member opportunity to make use of the positive skills and abilities which he possesses.

The older person who is ill in body or in spirit. This is a time of great testing. The older person is engaged in the inward battle where negative and positive forces sway him one way and then the other way. A warm, personal concern on the part of the people of the congregation is very important. There is need for alertness, too, to the need of professional services like that of the doctor or psychiatrist so that together, with pastor and people, there is a team approach.

A good book for the pastor's study and for the library of the congregation, which describes the processes related to aging is valuable. A recommended volume, written in a practical way, is *How to Help Older People* by Julietta K. Arthur. (See the Bibliography.)

When Do We Visit?

On a regular basis. The older person, especially if he is under duress, looks forward to such contact. Personal self-respect is involved, for regular visits from pastor and people buttress the older member with the feeling that he is remembered, worth while; and he also takes pains in preparing himself for such visitation.

At special times: When significant changes take place in his life. During special seasons and days of the church year which are more than ordinary in nature.

The older member may have his wrinkles and his waning abilities. These can be looked on either as the battle stripes of life or as the marks of retrogression. Much depends on the attitude. It is not aging itself but how aging is met that contributes to, or detracts from, life.

Where Do We Visit?

In the home of the older person.

In the Home for the Aged, if this is the place of residence.

In a nursing home, should such need arise for the older person.

In the hospital when such emergency exists.

Just so we visit—and visit regularly! The isolation that many older people experience is heightened for them under circumstances of need for personal services, especially when this necessitates residence in a special facility among new and strange surroundings.

Our visit needs to be person-centered. This means that we meet the person at his level of need and concern, not at ours.

Our visit will have the aim of making the person feel that we are concerned about him. It should be remembered that this concern includes all of the needs of the total person—body, mind, and spirit.

Our visit will have the point of making the ill person aware that God cares for him. The minister and the members of the congregation are in a good position to do this, for they are representatives of the congregation of which he is a part and of God, who, in Christ, is their mutual hope and life.

Our visits should be planned, and the framework of our planning can be based on notes we have taken on previous visits. These notes should record the actual conversations we have had with the ill. Studying these notes reveals where we ourselves were not as sensitive to the patient's needs as we might have been. Our planning should not be so concrete, however, that the plan is the purpose of the visit and the patient is secondary.

Some Physical Aspects of Visiting

Respect the rules of the home or hospital.

Make contact with the doctor, or nurse, to know the patient's condition. Such information is not, however, carried to the patient.

Watch that the bed is not bumped. The visitor should not sit on the bed, even if the patient may use it for that purpose.

Seated, or standing, our position should be one of consideration for the comfort of the patient.

Familiarity with the patient's needs and condition will help the visitor feel at ease. Tenseness is communicated to the patient and breeds tenseness.

Sudden movements, swift changes of tempo, sudden loudness, etc. can be surprising or startling to the patient and therefore upsetting.

Whispering with anyone within the range of sight or hearing of the patient contributes to his uneasiness.

Any reaction to sights, odors or expressions of the patient should not be revealed.

There is no such thing as a proper length of visit. The patient is watched for this clue.

Some Functional Aspects of Visiting

The approach to the ill (whether physical, emo-

tional, or spiritual) person calls for alertness as to
what the person has been experiencing. This includes
all personal objects in the room and any indication
of their use. It includes the dress of the person and
his physical appearance. It includes an appraisal of
the mood which the patient manifests.

The usual method of approach, "How are you?"
can be altered with good result. For example, seeing
a patient downcast, we may say, "You are downcast
today." This brings the visitor and the visitee together so that the patient is moved to the feeling that
his caller understands and is close to him.

The visitor will not carry his particular mood into
the visiting situation but will be concerned about the
mood of the patient.

The caller endeavors to find the edge of the patient's concerns. This means starting with the patient at his level of awareness.

The visitor encourages the patient to talk about
himself.

The visitor listens to the patient for mood and feelings. He also listens to the content of what the patient has been saying. The caller then asks himself:
What do these statements imply? The visitor then
takes note of his own feelings, thoughts, and observations and decides on his response. A patient's moods
or feelings should not be denied. He should be helped
to express his true feelings. Thus the caller will avoid
"instructing " or "preaching to" the patient as to how
he should feel or should not feel.

Scripture and prayer are resources for the visitor and patient. They will not be used just as part of the visit but when the caller has discovered the moods, feelings, and needs of the patient he will be able to select the Scripture which fits the patient and the content of the prayer will include what the patient has voiced. Thus Scripture and prayer are not meant to "control" the ill person but to help him.

THE ROLE OF FAITH FOR THE AGING

The Christian faith is relative to and has influence on the *entire* man—body, mind, and spirit. Yet, it is in the spirit of the man that the vital link with the living God is effected.

It is for this very reason that the Christian faith is of such importance to the older person. Physical strength may wane and mental ability decline but the spirit may continue its maturation and even grow to new heights. The significance of this is that one of the greatest privileges of older people is to know God, to love him and to serve him.

Older people do not, however, become more spiritual just because they grow older. It is what has been built into life, through the years, which the senior brings to his older years. If he has sought those things which are above he will possess them in his later years; and if he hasn't sought them before, they will not mean much to him when he is old and gray-headed. This does not mean that a man, by the Spirit of God, cannot come to his Savior and God in his late years, but his feelings for such need lessen as he lives through the years apart from God.

Old age with physical waning and mental decline and without spiritual balance is empty and meaningless. Faith helps the older person to face loss, to find reason for his existence, and to think of all of life as a part of his calling by God to relationship with him and man. A true faith in God brings the realization that the meaning of life is not found in mere outward activity but in inward growth. What does this suggest? It suggests:

That the church deliver the testimony of God in a clear voice and manner.

That the church, beginning with the young, teach the importance of Christian faith in preparing for and living the older years.

That the church reassure its older people with uninterrupted Christian services.

That the church enlarge its area of responsibility to its older people.

Fellowship for

THE OLDER PERSON

There are certain aspects of old age that must be taken into consideration by the congregation in planning a program for its older members.

One aspect is the curtailment of activity on the part of the seniors. Where once they had much activity in homemaking, rearing a family, and daily labor, now, in later years, they are finished with these roles. Workers with older people are aware of the frequent plaint: "I don't have anything to do." A number of reasons could be cited for this, and they would underscore the literalness and volume of this plaint. When a person has nothing to exercise body or mind he is sure to suffer loss of function in body and mind.

Another aspect of old age is loneliness. At every period in life personal well-being is dependent upon meaningful relationship to others; this is more so in the older years because of the losses which are suffered then. It is like dying by inches to be relegated to the "one-man's land" of loneliness.

There is a relation between activity and loneliness. Activity merely for the sake of activity becomes mechanical and does not satisfy. Activity, to be satisfying, must be with and for others. Neither is loneliness overcome simply by bringing a number of people together. There needs to be purpose to their being together so that, in carrying out that purpose, there is conveyed to each the feeling that he has need for others and that others need him.

We know:

That some older people are occupied.

That some older people are active.

That some older people have interesting chores.

That some older people have intriguing hobbies.

We also know:

That many have only a degree of occupation, activity, interesting chores, and hobbies.

That many are led, in their activity or loneliness, to brooding and frustration.

The congregation can help its older members in their time of loneliness and inactivity, by providing for the formation of fellowship groups where they can have rewarding experiences. Such fellowship groups may be called by various names, as: Golden Age

Club, Senior Fellowship, Never-Retired Club, Old But Still Busy, Growing Older Club, Lively Seniors.

BENEFITS OF A CLUB PROGRAM

Companionship. This is a need of all people, but it is probably felt most widely by older people because they are the ones, more than others, who have lost spouse, relatives, friends, neighbors.

Fellowship. We all have need of sharing our joys and sorrows, our thoughts and feelings, our needs and fulfillments. This, too, is a need of the older members of the congregation.

Occupation. People want to be engaged in interesting, helpful, and joyful activity. This is true also of older people.

Having fun together. This is an experience that has definite relation to health, appetite, digestion, and circulation. It is good medicine!

Sharing with others. Meager social contacts bring about slow, but certain, entrance to the ranks of lonely people.

Release of tensions. Tensions can easily rise and become ominous as there is a shift in living from active competitive roles to retirement and lessening of stimulating activity.

Thus it can be seen that experiences which will satisfy these needs are essential, and they can be provided for the older members of the congregation. The congregation can, if it has the will to do so, provide opportunity for fellowship programs. In doing this happiness will be added to the lives of seniors—adding the alloy which will help to make their declining years golden years.

Mrs. A. lives alone. She does not like it that way, but the circumstances of her life have made it so. Her marriage was not a successful one, and it was not her experience to know the companionship of a spouse, or to have children grow up around her in a setting of home and family. Even in early years she had to make her living, and through the years, by jobs of various kinds, she maintained her place of living and herself. She never had much opportunity, therefore, to form lasting friendships. Now, in later years, she has little companionship. Recently, by death, she lost her brother, and now just one sister remains who, however, lives at a distance and is ill. Sometimes she tries to find companionship among her neighbors, but they are mostly younger people. They are friendly enough, but they are busy with their children and their homes. Then, too, they don't seem to feel that they have much in common with an older woman. So Mrs. A. was pining for companionship. One day she was invited to a meeting of the Golden Age Club at the Center in her community. She went, and that did it! From that time on she lived a happier life because she found companionship. She looks forward to the meetings because she can spend her time in companionship with people who understand her needs because they have similar needs. In fact, the companionship has become so fruitful that now several of the club members visit each other in their homes. It was the fellowship program which brought them together and supplied their need of companionship.

Mr. S. is 70. He was always a busy man. As a young man he worked in the coal mines. To add to his meager income he did barbering on the side. With youth behind him he decided to quit the mining, move to the city, and barber full time. Up until five years ago he made his living this way and supported wife and child through the years. But five years ago he fell in his shop, breaking his hip. He was never able to return to his shop, nor find other employment. Mr. S., however, is a man who needs occupation, activity, and he found it in the Golden Age Club. He is the president now, and in the activity of the club he has found an outlet for his desire to be occupied with interesting and engaging projects. He hardly ever misses the meetings, but when he does we know it is because he is not feeling well. He said one day, "This club has filled a real need in my life."

Mrs. H. comes to club meetings regularly. Sometimes there is a far-away look in her eyes—almost sad. The leader of the club is conscious of this and asks Mrs. H. about it and usually Mrs. H. will say something like this, "I just get the blues sometimes from living alone. I have to talk to someone." She was not used to living alone. She came from a large family and she had a large family of her own, but now her husband is gone and her children have families of their own. Some live in distant cities. She visits, for a time, with this one and with that one, and then she comes home to her little apartment again. That's when the blues come. She wants to talk to someone, to share her thinking with them. She started coming to the Golden Age Club for that very reason, and it has supplied what she needs—free expression and sharing with others. You can tell she is a woman who needs such opportunity, for she is a lively participant in the club program and in her relationship with others who attend the club. She said one time, "I don't know what I would do if I did not have this club and these people."

STARTING A CLUB

Once the picture of the older people in the congregation comes into sharp focus, and a decision is made to start a club, the question arises: How does one begin? The initial step is the action taken by some key person. It is this person who, so to speak, unlocks the door to the planning room. In the congregation this can be the pastor or an interested lay person with whose help a good beginning is assured.

HOW THE PASTOR MAY HELP

Refer again, in this booklet, to the needs of older people (page 28). Make use of a survey in the congregation and study the results. Review, on page 68, the benefits of a fellowship program.

Present the needs of older people and the benefits of a fellowship program to the church board. Invite a decision for a club program in the congregation.

Select an organization in the congregation (this may be the committee spoken of on page 44) which will be understanding. Discuss the club project with this group. Seek to enlist the organization as a sponsor of the club project. (Read ahead to "How the

Sponsoring Organization May Help," page 74). Continuing consultation will be helpful to the sponsoring organization as it "plans" the strategy.

Consult with the sponsoring organization on ways to explore the congregation and the community for enrollment of members in the club project. (Read ahead to "Promoting a Club," page 77.)

Consult with the sponsoring organization to assist in securing a leader. (Reading ahead will reveal notes on "The Leader," page 79.)

Consult with the sponsoring organization so that plans will be made for volunteer drivers who can transport those who are in need of such assistance. (Farther ahead notes will be found on "The Volunteer Driver," page 82.)

The first meeting will be an event, a new venture in the congregation. You won't want to miss it! Expressions of the pastor's interest will be meaningful. This guiding note may be offered here: The usual experience is that club programs begin with small groups, and that the group builds up slowly. Likely the reason for this is that our social patterns of the past did not require provisions of this sort. Moreover, many older people are slow to try something new. Much patience will be necessary.

The pastor will drop in on meetings from time to time. The sponsors and club members will appreciate the interest shown. At such times the pastor can make contributions in an informal manner.

The presence of persons who are not members of the congregation cannot be used as a proselyting opportunity. There may be opportunity, however, to form contacts which will lead to giving help to the unchurched. A club program, providing a setting of Christian love and human warmth, may give occasion for fruitful contacts. These the pastor can make.

In human relations, problems sometimes come to light. Such may occur in a fellowship, or club, program. There is a likelihood that this will happen. The pastor, as a group worker, will help in finding solutions which are in keeping with the best interests of the club and the church.

The pastor is a busy person. It could seem that a club program would be just another responsibility added to the many others. However, the pastor will find that the increasing number of older people has already confronted him with a responsibility, and so he may see some of that responsibility discharged in a club program.

In the early stages of the club program the pastor may have to be the initiator. His promotive leadership will be very important. As the program takes shape the pastor will then find it valuable to withdraw to the role of advisor and interested helper. A group that manages its own program becomes a source of joy to the pastor. Also, as he sees how meaningful the program has become to the participants he will enjoy the rewards his efforts have produced.

THE SPONSORING ORGANIZATION MAY HELP

By assisting the pastor. After his initial planning is under way he will need aid from an interested, organized group within the congregation.

By assisting the church board. The board, after evaluating a club program and seeking to inaugurate such a service, will need the acceptance by a group within the congregation to assume guiding responsibility.

By accepting the challenge. The pastor needs the assistance of a sponsoring group, and the church board's official action can be implemented by the availability of a sponsoring group. The older members and their needs are at stake. Implementation now comes through a wider acceptance of responsibility.

By offering financial support. Such support will be required mainly for the initial stages of the club development. While the planning and organization are taking place there will be some items of cost. These will not be prohibitive. Once a club is a reality, there usually is a desire on the part of the membership to be contributing.

By providing a general committee. It need not be large, but care should be taken that an older person, or persons, be included in the membership. Working with the pastor and its own sponsoring organization steps like these can be taken:

Secure a leader. (See page 79.)

Secure volunteers to recruit members for the club. (See page 78.)

Make arrangements to supply mimeographed copies of "This Is Your Invitation." (See page 81.)

Determine factors like date, time, age, and sex for the initial club meeting.

Attend the initial club meeting, providing needed materials and lunch, consulting with and helping the leader.

Provide a supply of reminder cards for subsequent meetings. Later the club can assume the responsibility.

Provide a supply of birthday cards. Later the club can assume the responsibility.

Provide blank membership cards for record purposes. (3-in. by 5-in. index cards are good.)

Provide copies of an information card and interest data sheet for the use of the leader. Here is a guide:

INFORMATION ABOUT MEMBER

Name................... Address.................
Phone......... Birthday........ Occupation.........
Check: Married... Single... Widow... Widower...
Member of what church?...........................
Do you live with someone?.........................
Whom? ....
Do you need transportation to the place of meetings?...

INTEREST DATA

What do you like? What do you like to do?
We all want our club to serve us and we want to

get as much out of it as we can. One way of doing this is to have some expression from you about your likes and wants. So, check below:

Hobbies—I would like to know more about:
.... Making models (cars, planes, boats, houses . . .)
.... Crafts (wood, leather, metal, clay . . .)
.... Scrapbooks.... Coin collecting
.... Stamp collecting .... Knitting, embroidering
.... Painting .... Gardening .... Dramatics
.... Things I can make to sell for extra income
Other ....
Speakers—I would enjoy speakers on subjects like:
.... Travel .... Making a will .... Employment
.... Retirement pointers .... Health problems
.... Educational opportunities .... Government
.... Historical places .... Social security
Other ....
Games—What kind do you like?
.... Table games, like checkers, bingo . . .
.... Games of an active kind, like shuffleboard
.... Group games .... Any kind
Outdoor activities:
.... Picnics .... Trips to parks, beauty spots
.... Trips to museums, art centers, industries
List others ....
....

Confer with the sponsoring organization to arrange for volunteer drivers who will transport club members needing such assistance.

Make arrangements to supply the leader with copies of "Relationship to Sponsoring Organization." (See page 84.)

Pray with your planning. This is a new venture, but much is expected of it. No one can predict the benefits accruing to the seniors. Let the Lord direct the planning of the committee.

PROMOTING A CLUB

Suggestions will be found below for the Sponsoring Organization relative to finding prospects, recruiting them, leadership, volunteer drivers, and the like.

Finding Prospects

1. Consult with the pastor.

2. Make use of the membership roll.

3. Contact organizations in the community, expanding beyond the membership of the congregation and thus serving the community.

4. Consult the physicians in the community for names of older persons whom they know and who would benefit from group experiences.

5. Call the Aid for Aged offices for names of those who are known to need the benefits offered in a club program.

6. Call the Rest Homes in the community, consulting with the supervisor about the older people there who would benefit through a supervised program.

7. Invite the public library to furnish information about some older people who frequent the library, some of whom probably would welcome the opportunity of participation.

8. Contact service clubs in the community.

9. Inquire among personal acquaintances. Through such leads information can be obtained about new arrivals in the community—for instance an older person who comes to live with a son or daughter.

Recruiting Prospects

1. Have volunteers make personal calls on the predetermined number of prospects.

2. Have volunteers explain the club program to the prospects, citing the benefits of the club program.

3. Supply the prospects with a copy of "This Is Your Invitation." (See page 81.)

4. Give a warm personal invitation.

5. Repeat the place, date, and time of meetings as found in the copy of "This Is Your Invitation."

6. Make arrangements for transportation, if this is necessary.

7. Offer to accompany the prospect to the first meeting.

Advertising the Initial Meeting

1. Supply the date for the church bulletin.

2. Have the pastor make a personal announcement.

3. Ask community organizations to make announcements.

4. Place notices in store windows, etc.

5. Use the community newspapers. Have some information included about the purpose of the club program.

The Leader

The leader is the central figure in the formation of a club. However, lest this frighten any prospect for leadership, let it be noted that the leader is the central figure in the beginning stages; later, as the club develops, members are drawn into the places of activity and leadership. As club members "take over," the leader moves into the background and becomes cooperator and advisor. In this way the leader encourages the members of the group to become active participants.

The leader will, in the early stages, probably have to double as activities director and recreational director, but the plan will be to have the members assume roles they can handle—helping themselves, running the club. Little by little, then, the leader

becomes more a helper, an associate, and interested
guide.

Some qualifications to be taken into consideration
in selecting a leader:

A leader manifests the Christian spirit.

A leader sees the older person as one of God's own
design and works with him as a fellow person of
God's making.

A leader approaches his work with older people as
a privilege, not as a task to be done. In God's economy it is always a privilege to serve those with whom
we are working.

A leader promotes optimism, friendliness, and gen-
erosity by personal example.

A leader keeps trying, learning by mistakes, profit-
ing by progressive experience.

A leader is considerate enough of others to see that
everyone within a group is equally and fairly treated.

While these qualifications of a leader may seem
to be many in number and of special significance,
they are found in many of our church members. In
other words, a sensible, earnest, interested, concerned
Christian person is the kind we want for a leader,
and many such are to be found in our congregations.

It would, of course, be good if a leader could be
found who is a trained group worker, but this is by
no means necessary. What is very important is that
he be a dedicated person who possesses the Christian
spirit, is interested in older people and is willing to

make use of the abilities and talents he has. Such a person, walking with the Lord and loving those with whom he works, is indeed a leader to be desired.

This Is Your Invitation

(Suggested copy of an invitation, for promoting the club, to those who are contacted for enrollment in the club program.)

Life has been slipping by, hasn't it?

You have had many good experiences.

You have had a part also in the disappointments and discouragements that are a part of life.

You have been active and energetic.

And God has been with you in so many ways through the years. You have felt his love in Christ and experienced his comfort and guidance through the Holy Spirit. With his help you have lived and labored and loved to this day.

However, each day has lengthened your life, and now you have joined the ranks of our older people. Hats off to you! There are many of you! God bless you!

AS AN OLDER PERSON YOU SHARE IN EXPERIENCES LIKE THESE:

In retirement or semi-retirement you have more time on your hands than you have been used to through the years.

There is inactivity because a career, or job, is no longer being followed.

You experience loneliness because spouse, friends, or neighbors have been slipping away.

There is less mingling with others because of lack of

transportation, health problems, lack of companions, etc., thus giving you little opportunity for common worship experiences, sharing of ideas, fellowship, or recreation.

Consider these questions:

Are you often lonely?

Do you have time on your hands when you find that there is not much that needs to be done?

Would you like to be in the company, occasionally, of friends of your own age?

Do you miss opportunities of sharing with others the experiences that come to you?

Would you like to have some fun with people your own age?

Would you like to meet with older people who have the same kind of experiences and feelings?

Surely you would, since you are like the rest of us. So this is your invitation:

ATTEND THE FIRST MEETING
OF A CLUB FOR OLDER PEOPLE

THE PLACE ....

THE DATE ....

THE TIME ....

WHO IS ELIGIBLE? Anyone, men, women, 60 or over. The aim is to bring together the older persons of the congregation and the community that they may find companionship, enjoy recreation, take part in interesting programs, and share in services to God and to others. In such interests club members will find opportunities for a fuller, happier life as they live their golden years.

SUGGESTIONS FOR VOLUNTEER DRIVERS

You have volunteered to be a driver to provide transportation for older persons who have no mode of conveyance to club meetings. This is a service of real importance. Without your help some older persons might not be able to take part in a club program who would like to do so. The service you give will help to provide many happy hours for some older people.

You will, however, want to do more than just drive. You will also want to be mindful of suggestions like those which follow:

Be on time. If the appointed time has arrived and you are not there, the older person may become upset. If haste must then be made to arrive at the meeting place on time, this too can be disturbing. Late arrival may even affect the person's ability to enter into club activities with calm and ease.

Be helpful. The older person may need help on steps, at street crossings, or getting in and out of the car. Avoid being too solicitous but be ready to give a hand whenever there is a need for such help.

Be dependable. The club function may be one of the few opportunities the older person has for getting away from home, experiencing a change, finding a medium of exchange with others. It would be a great disappointment to be forced to cancel it because you have failed.

Supply a substitute if and when you cannot drive. Preparation should be made for just such a possibility by having a volunteer who can take your place when the need arises.

Be cheerful. A cheerful disposition is catching.

Practice it as you drive the older person to the meeting.

Be courteous. It's a natural social grace, of course, but more than that, it's a way of showing respect for the aged. This will always be appreciated.

Be a good driver. Traffic problems and traffic hazards can be upsetting to anyone. They probably are more so to older people. Speed can be very disturbing to aged persons. Drive carefully! Drive safely!

RELATIONSHIP TO SPONSORING ORGANIZATION

(Copies of the following may be provided for each enrollee, or be used as a guide for discussion to help members to an understanding of their club's responsibility to their sponsor.)

The church has a deep, abiding interest in you. This is true because the church is concerned about human beings and wants to serve them in the name of the living and redeeming Christ.

An indication of this interest is that the people of the church offer the facilities of the church so that some of those needs may be met. As you take part in a club program in the environment of the church it is hoped that your desire for fellowship, friends, activity, and the overcoming of loneliness will be satisfied. Various problems which may come to you will also be of interest to the church and you are invited to seek help at any time.

Keep in mind, then, that the church is the sponsor of your club and has inaugurated, within the congregation, a program of fellowship among seniors because it is believed that you will find benefit in such a program.

Of course you and your fellow club members are aware of this and likely, as a club, you may want to *show* your awareness. Perhaps you would like to know what you can do, as a club, to indicate your appreciation. It is with this in mind that some suggestions are offered in the following lines. They are in the way of procedures which could be followed.

1. Upon the organization of your club you could draw up a letter of thanks and send it to the church, expressing how you feel about the congregation's interest in your behalf in providing the facilities for your club meetings.

2. The officers of your club, and you as members, can strive always to cooperate with the pastor and the official board of the church.

3. The officers of your club, and you as members, can show your appreciation by close cooperation with the organization in the congregation which is sponsoring your club.

4. The church has certain principles by which it is guided. By respecting these and complying with them you will be indicating your appreciation. This

will mean that at all times programs will be followed which are in harmony with these principles.

5. Your appreciation can also be shown by attendance at other functions of the church, like worship services. If you are a member of the congregation, you know the joy of worshipping with your fellow members. If you are a member of another congregation, you will not want to miss the opportunity to worship there, and if you are not a member of any church, the opportunity of worship is extended to you.

What about the club program? This is a pressing question. Once you set the stage for a program and you bring the older people together, what are you going to do? Whether the meeting is of long or short duration you will want to know what to do in the time you have.

OUTLINE OF CLUB PROGRAM

1. *Assembly.* The hour of meeting is set but the members will be arriving at various intervals before this. Lest the pre-meeting time become a period of uncertainty, fidgeting and the like, previously selected hostesses can take the lead in getting people acquainted and chatting with each other in an informal manner.

2. *Group Participation* can get the meeting under way, such as:

Singing, always popular, and don't overlook the old favorites. Imagination can produce variation.

An organized mixer to bring each person into activity.

Group recital of the flag pledge.

Group reading, or recitation, from mimeographed manuscripts. This could also be done from memory by previous arrangement.

3. Recognition Time

Introducing newcomers.

Recognizing birthdays.

Recognizing acts of service and current accomplishments on the part of the attenders.

Inviting individuals to tell what they have been reading, studying, observing, doing, etc. Encourage each individual to stand in the limelight in some way.

4. *Devotional Period.* Should there be a spiritual element, a period used for devotions through Scripture, prayer, and meditation? This will depend on the membership. If the members are all of the local congregation, this may be a definite desire. Should the membership be a mixed group, it may be that a definite period for spiritual expression will not be a foregone conclusion at all. Let the group decide whether a specific period for spiritual devotion is desired. If so, this can be handled in various ways. It may be a part of the regular program or it may be a prelude

to the meeting itself. With a mixed group some kind of voluntary participation could be developed.

5. *Activities.* The activities period is the backbone of the meeting. The greatest amount of time is employed in activities of various kinds. Minds will be active and hands will be busy. Thus a basic purpose of the club is furthered, to fill the hours of older people so that time will not hang so heavily. Activity is splendid therapy. Tremendous latitude is possible in the realm of club activity. A program can be devoted to a single broad type or to any combination of activities.

Types possible are:

Physical—games of various kinds.

Mental—forums, discussions, lectures.

Recreative—picnics, outings, parties, trips.

Special—various projects to help church and community organizations.

Hobbies—For personal enjoyment and possible remuneration as well as individual participation in hobby shows.

Thus a club program could be centered in one type of activity at a given meeting, a different type at another, or it could be one of variety. Whatever is done, rigidity needs to be avoided and club members must be given the opportunity to express their desires about the type of activity in which they wish to engage.

Fear of the lack of ideas for a program of activities need never be a factor. There are many possibilities. Consider the long list which follows here:

Indoor Activities

Art	Millinery
Bowling	Model making
Cards	Movies
Chair caning	Painting
Checkers	Parties
Chess	Photography
China painting	Playreading
Community sing	Poetry
Concerts	Pottery
Crafts	Public speaking
Creative writing	Quilting
Crocheting	Radio
Dramatics	Reading
Dressmaking	Service programs
Forum	Sewing
Games	Stamp collecting
Glee club	Swimming
Holiday celebrations	Variety band
Home nursing	Weaving
Jewelry making	Whittling
Leatherwork	Woodcarving
Lectures	

Outdoor Activities

Archery	Croquet
Auto rides	Curling
Baseball	Deck tennis
Boat rides	Flycasting
Bocci	Fishing
Bowling	Gardening
Calisthenics	Golf (miniature)
Camping	Geology

Horseshoes
Hunting
Hikes
Picnics
Quoits
Riding
Roque
Rowing
Sailing

Shooting
Shuffleboard
Softball
Swimming
Skating
Table tennis
Trips
Volleyball
Walking

Other Activities

Newspaper editing
Birthday parties
Amateur shows

Folk dances
Festivals
Discussions

Thus one can start with an art and end with wood-carving, or start with archery and end with walking. In between, practically every letter of the alphabet suggests an activity program.

Consider these program suggestions:

Making dressings for the Cancer Society.
Working on Red Cross assistance projects.
Preparing layettes for the underprivileged.
Repairing toys for Christmas.
Making scrap books for rest homes.
Making holiday cards for Children's Hospitals.
Visiting in local rest homes.
Visiting among the aged and shut-in in the neighborhood.
Helping with the service projects of an organization in the community, or of the sponsoring congregation.

There are always books from which ideas and guidance can be gleaned. The public library is a good source for such volumes, as are publishing houses. The seeker might look for these:

Fun for Older Adults, by Helen and Larry Eisenberg. Tennessee Book Co., Nashville, Tenn. ($1).

Recreation in the Senior Years, by Arthur M. Williams. Association Press, New York ($3.95).

Recreational Activity Development for the Aging in Homes, Hospitals, and Nursing Homes, by Carol Lucas. C. C. Thomas, Pub., Springfield, Ill. ($4.25).

Recreation in Church and Community, edited by Warren T. Powell. Abingdon Press, Nashville, Tenn. ($1.25).

Fun for Older Adults, by Virginia Stafford and Larry Eisenberg. Methodist Publishing House, Nashville, Tenn.

The Fun Encyclopedia and Gay Parties. Abingdon Press, Nashville, Tenn.

Helping Older People Enjoy Life, by James H. Woods. Harpers, New York.

Active Games and Contests, by Bernard Mason and Elmer Mitchell. Ronald Press, New York.

The Book of Games, by G. Sherman Ripley. Association Press, New York.

Games for All Occasions, by Ken Anderson and Morry Carlson. Zondervan Publishing House, Grand Rapids, Mich.

Games for Quiet Hours and Small Spaces, National Recreation Association, New York.

Games the World Around Us — Four Hundred Folk Games, by Sarah Ethridge Hunt and Ethel Cain. Ronald Press, New York.

Arts and Crafts, by Marguerite Ickis. A. S. Barnes and Co., New York.

Handcraft publication can be secured from The National Recreation Association, 315 Fourth Ave., New York.

6. *Refreshments*

To eat, or not to eat? Whenever this question is considered in a club program there is the usual affirmative answer. Eating seems to be a part of our bountiful American way of life. Older people enjoy it. Besides, having more time on their hands than the average person, older people find the usual pleasure in chatting with their companions as they are congregated for refreshments.

The food need not be substantial. It is the occasion of being together rather than the amount of food which is supportive to a successful program. Moreover, there is good opportunity to have members contribute their favorite refreshment dish. At each meeting a selected member might be asked to present his "Special."

A variation of the whole club program in relation to hours of meeting and refreshment could be a potluck, with members contributing their favorites and expounding on their favorite recipes.

7. *Cleaning up.*

Here everyone can give a helping hand.

AIMS TO KEEP IN MIND

That a program be conducted *with* club members and not *for* them.

That everyone be drawn into some kind of activity during the club program.

That club members be drawn into activity between the meetings supportive to the club program.

That the club be a leisure time and leisure activity situation for the members so that none are used and none are pressured.

The above lines for a club program are only suggestive: Any group in any community is urged to adopt any workable plan. But whatever the program, let the members take part in a mood of informality and relaxation.

Keeping Club Members Active

A good guiding principle is: "Never do for a club member what he can do for himself." Interest is heightened sharply by participation and responsibility. The following suggestions may serve as examples of responsibilities which can be delegated:

Sending out notices.

Welcoming members at the door.

Serving as host and hostess.

Working on entertainment committee.

Serving on membership committee to call on prospects.

Preparing refreshments, or serving them.

Decorating and cleaning up.

Acting in the role of
—Librarian of books and magazines.
—Secretary for the records.
—Treasurer for different funds.
—Membership secretary to contact absent members.

Let the Group Make Decisions

What is to be the name of the club?

How often and at what hours should meetings be held?

What is to be the program?

Are there to be dues or contributions?

How are collected funds to be used?

SOME DIRECTIVES

No formal organization takes place in the starting stages of the club.

Members are those of the age specified by the sponsoring organization committee (60 years or more is suggested, but this need not be firm) who will fill out registration cards and attend.

The size of the group is not too important.

The leader forms committees to assume the first responsibilities within the group: program, membership, refreshments, etc.

After the club has met a number of times an organizational structure just naturally begins to take shape. The specific needs show up and the people best fitted are found to meet them.

Officers and committee members should not function in their capacities too long. Short terms are best, quarterly or half-year periods.

Any constitution should be very simple. The name, aim, times of meetings, officers and their duties, will suffice. The usual rules of order are important.

Dues are received only if the group itself wants it this way. The limited ability of some older people to contribute needs to be kept in mind. The best manner of collection would probably be a collection box in some convenient place, and participation should be wholly voluntary.

Let all who are in leadership capacity move into the background as they succeed in bringing club members into the foreground.

Wherever possible think and work in terms of *group* activity rather than individual, isolated effort. Make use of individual effort, but let it be a means of bringing others into group participation. Lead members into the joy of serving others.

The Word, Christ, the church, worship—these are basic. Add to them a club program for the older members of the congregation. This is another way to augment the program of the church in bringing to the older people fulfillment of their basic needs.

A club program among the older members of the congregation can help:

To promote mental alertness.

To retard the processes of disintegration as older people become inactive or handicapped.

To provide in the group a substitute for the family as family members pass away or are widely removed, bringing acceptance and love.

To provide opportunities for self-expression and creativeness.

Visitors' Service for

THE OLDER PERSON

Every congregation knows about:

The widow who lives alone.

The aged man who has nothing to do.

The ill member who seldom sets foot outside his house, isolated from others.

The infirm member, not trusting himself to leave the familiarity of his dwelling place.

The shut-in at a local rest home, ill and lonely from day to day, apart from others.

Every congregation has:

The member who is looking for something to do.

The member who, because of retirement, has time on his hands.

The member who, because the busy family role has passed, is ready to give his attention to personal interest.

The member who is willing to act in a volunteer role.

Within the congregation those members who will find the time, are deeply interested and concerned, can be directed to go to older members who are shut-in, home-bound, lonely, or ill. In this way a Christian service is rendered.

It will benefit those who receive.

It will benefit those who give.

It will bring together those who need each other, each growing in the feeling of the significance of life when there is a mutual element of care motivated by the Gospel of Jesus Christ

Friendly visiting is what we call this activity, an activity practiced in the church from the day of its beginning.

The Scriptures teach us:

"Bear one another's burdens."

"Comfort one another."

"Contribute to the needs of the saints, practice hospitality."

CAN YOU QUALIFY AS A FRIENDLY VISITOR?

The idea of friendly visiting may seem foreign to you, or strange, and you may think that only one who has special training can do such work. Such fears need not deter you. To qualify as a friendly visitor requires only that one be an average person, willing to use his native ability and ready to serve older people. Also, some helpful guidance can always be had to assist one for preparation as a friendly visitor.

YOU CAN QUALIFY BECAUSE

You can pray and thus receive guidance and power from God. You can pray for the one you will visit that blessing may come to him through your willing service. Count on prayer as your great resource. The Lord will not leave you powerless in doing work in his name.

You can be generous, giving some of your time to bring cheer into the life of another, encouraging him to know that he is remembered.

You can be sociable, showing the one you are visiting that you enjoy being in his presence and sharing with him in his needs.

You can be helpful to one who has special requirements.

You can be yourself by simply showing another that you have genuine interest in him. Such interest will capture anyone, certainly our older people.

You can serve Jesus Christ, learning anew that you are ready to serve instead of being served.

PREPARATION FOR VISITING

Willingness to visit is a step in the direction of preparing yourself to take part in this service to the older members of the congregation.

Read material which is prepared to help those who want to be friendly visitors.

Attend meetings which are planned for the discussion of those things which will be helpful to the friendly visitor, learning the techniques of a successful visiting program.

Read about older people and get acquainted with their characteristics and needs. There are some books written for this purpose, like:

Older People and the Church ($2.50). Cedarleaf and Maves.
You Came Unto Me ($1.00). Russell Dicks.
When You Grow Older (25 cents). Public Affairs Pamphlet.
How to Help Older People ($4.95). Juliette K. Arthur.

Be prepared to give time and effort, which are necessary elements of friendly visiting. For this no awards will be handed out but you will always remember the joy and the pleasure which you noted on the part of those you visited.

"DO'S" OF FRIENDLY VISITING

Pray. Prayer is a great resource to personal preparation. It helps you to "decrease" so that someone else may "increase."

Consider your approach. Your attitude is very important. You do not enter this service because you are sorry for the visitee but because you want to learn and share the concerns of that person.

Be cheerful. Prepare yourself in the climate of cheerfulness. As you approach and enter the home of the person you are going to visit you will find that this spirit cuts through many moods you may find in others.

Tell the family, in a private home, why you want to visit. You need their understanding. In a rest home first contact the supervisor or owner, explaining what your interest is in calling. The owner can help you to be better informed about the experiences the visitee has been having.

Be friendly. Friendliness is infectious and wholesome. Your friendliness will be remembered. However, you must see that this is not overdone and you give the impression that it is "put on." Your friendliness must be genuine.

Be a listener, for older people, as a rule, want to talk to someone. Be a patient listener, for you will likely hear repeated what you have already heard several times before. Encourage their talking—it is a relieving therapy.

Be understanding, entering into the interests, moods, etc., of the person. You can give much reassurance this way.

Be watchful, however, that you do not take sides in the person's problems. Let him tell you about them, real or imaginary, but make no issue by taking a position "for" or "against" in the situation.

Keep to yourself all that has been shared with you. To betray confidences would destroy what has been built up. It would make the person on whom you are calling wary of trusting you again.

Establish your visits on a regular basis. Let the person know when you are coming again. He will be looking forward to it, planning for it.

Read a Scripture portion and have a prayer with the person you are visiting. This may be done at any time when the situation suggests it. Selection of material, however, is very important, so that what is read relates to his need. There are of course times when Scripture and prayer may not be called for, as for example, when you visit (as in a rest home) someone of a distinctly different faith, or no faith at all. You should not hold a person captive to your wish, nor force upon him what you believe should be good for him. You can inquire as to a person's feelings on this matter, but you will abide by his wishes.

Report to your pastor. Do it on a regular basis. It would be best to do this in writing. When you have special problems he will be able to help you. He will always be ready to give you helpful guidance also.

Send cards and little notes. Should you be visiting in a general situation, like in a rest home, it is best not to include your address in your correspondence, so that you may not set up some dependency situation. The person addressed can thank you personally on your visits.

Encourage the persons you visit to do something for others.

"DONT'S" OF FRIENDLY VISITING

Don't disappoint your visitee. You may never know how much your visit meant to him. Let there be a set date for the visit. If, for some reason, you cannot keep the date, inform your visitee about it, and make arrangements about the time of your next visit. Inattention to this procedure can contribute to a feeling of worthlessness on the part of the person you are visiting.

Don't be surprised at anything told you by the visitee or by anyone related to him. You may be, but don't show it.

Don't feel sorry for the person, "sighing" and "oh-ing" with him. This can lead to depression. Be emotionally neutral, not too warm or too cold, but intensely interested.

Don't condemn any action or speech on the part of the person you are visiting. You are a visitor and not a judge who says, "You are wrong" or, "I would not do that."

Don't give advice, allowing the person to depend on you as a crutch. You will want to help him do his own deciding. Suggest alternatives to him. When he makes his own decision he is helping himself. It adds to ego strength.

Don't enter into debates. Controversial subjects can lead to disagreement and hard feelings. This is not the role of a friendly visitor. Just be a listener, leading the person to talk about himself.

Don't take the "rose-colored glasses" approach, assuring that everything is going to be all right. This only buries the person's feelings or problems. Encourage him to talk so that he is able to unburden himself.

Don't dominate the situation. Do not take charge so that you say, "Today we are going to do this" or, "I decided we would try this today." By this method you center attention on yourself when it is the person you are visiting who is to have the attention.

Don't be shocked at anything you see. The person you are visiting has his own rights, even though he may be doing what you would not do.

Don't show reaction to anything unpleasant. There may be odor, bad breath, loose dentures. You have come to bring cheer, not to be critical.

Don't dwell on the woes of the world, like war, delinquency, murder, accident, and such.

Don't bring your problems with you. Leave them at the door. Bring radiance and reassurance.

Don't discontinue your visiting. When you must, tell the person why, otherwise he may think he is at fault and has done something that has offended you.

Don't forget to be a *"friendly"* visitor.

POINTERS ON REST HOME VISITING

First make contact with the owner or operator. Tell him why you want to come, namely, for friendly visiting.

Tell the operator you respect the operator-resident relationship and that you want to be careful not to disturb that in any way, but that, on the other hand, you feel that your service can add well-being to the resident and help him to adjust to his home away from home.

Be sure that you do no harm, in any way, to the resident-operator relationship.

Individual visiting is better than having a group make a "grand tour" approach. A whole group may indeed call in a home, but best results can be attained in the individual to individual approach.

Calling in a group, or as an individual, ask the operator which persons, in his estimation, are the best subjects for the visitation. The operator is best suited to tell you which persons need prior concern.

If the individual on whom you are calling is in a ward, first make a general, friendly approach to all who are in the room. Then gradually make your settled visit with the person you have come to see.

It will add to good relations to contact the operator at the beginning of each visiting period, and also at the conclusion. Express thankfulness for the opportunity you have had.

There are many rest homes in the community, as

a rule. For the residents, one day is much like the
other. A friendly visit will always be remembered.

THE FOLLOW-UP TO FRIENDLY VISITING

You will not be visiting very long before you find
that you have the feeling of wanting "to do something" for someone. It is just natural that, as a human, your feeling will go out to your fellow human.

Or you may find that someone will ask you to do
a special favor for him, like getting his "special" pills
or talking to someone for him. (This would be most
likely in a rest home, for the resident does not have
very much outside contact.)

What to do? If you start getting "things" for a resident you may become involved in something leading beyond your expectation. If you "talk to someone" for the patient you may contribute to harm.

What to do? Just remember:

You have come to visit.

You have come to bring human warmth.

You have come because you are concerned.

*You have come to show an older person that he is
worthwhile.*

Your responsibility? Just to be a friendly visitor.

WHAT TO DO ABOUT SPECIAL PROBLEMS

You will be calling on older people as a friendly
visitor to bring moments of pleasantness, understand-

ing, cheer, and genuine interest into their lives, whether they be in their own homes or in institutions. As you gain the friendship and interest of such older people you will find, possibly, that someone wants to confide in you about personal problems.

Remember, older people do have problems.

Some may say that:

No one ever bothers about them.

Their family has taken advantage of them.

They need medicine which they are not receiving.

They are not getting enough to eat.

Others talk about them or blame them for practically everything that happens.

They do not have enough clothing.

Their possessions have been stolen, or taken away from them.

Don't commit yourself to any action.

Don't take sides in the matter.

Don't express yourself about persons whose names may have been cited.

Just listen! Listen! Listen!

Help the person to empty himself of the subject he has introduced. However, if you consider the problem to be significant, then ask the person if you have his permission to discuss his problem with the proper person—the family, the pastor, the case worker, the operator, the doctor. If permission is granted, consult with the proper individual. In this way you will serve as part of a team in the interest of the older person.

Remember:

You are not calling as a *pastor.*
You are not calling as a *case-worker.*
You are not calling as a *relief-worker.*
You are not calling as a *problem solver.*
You are calling as a friendly visitor, to bring warmth, cheer and interest to an older person.

There is a wide variety of things which you can take with you for help, in your visiting.

Spiritual Helps

The Sunday church bulletin.
The denominational paper or magazine.
Bible recordings.
A recording of your Sunday worship service.
A filmstrip might be shown.
Photographs of activities in the congregation.
A devotional booklet.

Reading Material

Magazines, but be sure they are fairly current and of good print.
A favorite newspaper for a rest home resident.

Comic books—believe it or not, a number of older people like them.

A novel, of good print.

For Fun

A game of some kind.
Checkers, dominoes, scrabble, solitaire.
Portable phonograph and records.
Interesting photographs.
A picture puzzle.

For Activity

Writing letters.
Taking a walk. (In rest homes first clear with the supervisor.)
Going for a ride. (Clear, in rest homes.)
Working together on a simple craft.

Before You Go You Can Offer

To tidy the room, make the bed, shake the rugs.
To do the grocery shopping.
To make arrangements, for the next time, about making a visit to some favorite place.
To take the older member to the worship services.

Bring Older People to Church

As a friendly visitor you are the logical person to volunteer to bring seniors, at home or in a rest home, to your church for various activities.

Bring them for the worship services.

Bring them for special services: communion, Christmas, Easter, Mother's Day, Father's Day.

Recognize their presence. Point out that your church includes older people in its interests.

Bring them to a party. It can be general in nature, or a special one like Valentine Day, Halloween, birthday.

Bring them for a special meeting of a society. Some of them have probably been in an organization of the congregation and would find much enjoyment in an occasional meeting with the group. It would be a stimulating experience. Don't overlook having them take care of some of the less active, but important, parts of a meeting: records, telephoning, sunshine cards.

Bring them to a dinner—a dinner just for them. Or make them guests of honor at a congregational dinner, a family night. Such thoughtful action will be long remembered.

Bring them for a picnic, on the church grounds if need be but better yet at a public park, a shelter house, or an amusement park. Older people we have known have talked of such experiences again and again. They are worth while

OCCUPATION WITH SOME ACTIVITY

Most people have led busy and useful lives. For an older person it is unfortunate if no opportunity can be found to give outlet to activity desires.

Crafts, very simple in nature, can be constructive therapy, the means to activity; and activity recreates the mind.

Projects of societies in our congregations, or community organizations, may be used to enroll older members in some form of activity. Some possibilities:

A society in the congregation probably has a service project. Maybe clothing is made for use on a foreign mission field. Perhaps some society is sewing for one of the institutions of the church. Take material with you when you visit the older members. They can help, and in turn will feel that they are useful to others.

Your congregation may be planning a bazaar, holiday sales, etc. Take material to the older members and have them help, in their leisure hours, to prepare different articles. Their importance to others can be supported in this way.

The local Cancer Society might be contacted to see if help is needed in making dressings. Get the specifications and materials. Enlist the help of the members you are visiting. Explain what service they can be rendering.

Mend toys which have been collected for that purpose. These can be taken to a children's hospital or to the church's welfare organization. Older members will find joy in bringing a similar feeling to some youngsters. Such usefulness is recreative.

Make a scrapbook, a venture which can be undertaken by older shut-ins. Invite them to help in collecting pictures, articles, verses, etc., to be used in a scrapbook on a general theme, or a particular one like Christmas. Such scrapbooks can be offered to an institution in the area.

Crafts, in general, are fine opportunities to enlist the interest of older people. Of course, space is a factor in some instances, like in a rest home, but even bed patients can handle some crafts like flower-making, tray or table favors, pattern-making, weaving, knitting, and hand coloring. Favors that are made can be offered to local institutions to brighten the meals of an ill, but not forgotten, person.

Instead of giving directions which would require much space, a list of books giving helps, ideas, directions and patterns follows:

Diversions for the Sick (Simple crafts and projects). John Hancock Life Ins. Co., Boston. Free.

Handcraft with Dennison Crepe Paper. Dennison Manufacturing Co., Framingham, Mass. 25 cents.

101 Uses for Craft Strip. Ericksen's Crafts, 304 N. Main St., Hutchinson, Kansas. 29 cents.

Soap Carving (a pamphlet of instructions). National Soap Sculpture Comm., 160 Fifth Ave., New York. Free.

Nelly Bee Loom Weaving (for making slippers, pot holders, mats, bags, etc.). Nelly Bee Products, Hickory, N. C. 25 cents.

Activities in Nursing Homes (pointers for volunteers, suggestions for crafts and games). Div. of Public Assistance, State Dept. of Public Welfare, 801 Harrison, Topeka, Kansas.

Merrily We Play (50 party games for older people).
Education-Recreation Div. of Health and Welfare
Council, 311 S. Juniper Street, Philadelphia 7. 50 cents.

Various games and crafts pamphlets can be secured by
writing to Cooperative Recreation Service, Inc., Dela-
ware, Ohio. Cost is usually about 25 cents.

Instructor's Manual (Crafts). American Handicraft Store,
38 E. 14th St., New York.

A LAST WORD

Friendly visiting will require effort, but the effort
will go a long way toward meeting a challenge to
our society: to engage our older people in daily,
purposeful, active, interesting living. May the Lord
be your source of inspiration and strength as well as
your guide when you serve as a Friendly Visitor.

Friendly visiting is like a two-way street—the visitor gives a service and the one visited receives a
service, and both experience the benefit.

Mrs. K. has been an invalid for more than twenty
years. She is paralyzed from head to foot and in her im-
mobile condition cannot lie directly on her bed but is
slightly suspended over it in a hammock-like frame. Early
in her invalidism she purposely had her jawbones broken
to allow more room in her mouth so she might effect a
way to talk. On visiting her a person may begin to feel
sorry for her, but on leaving he will feel it is he who
has benefitted by the visit. She enters fully into conversation and gives evidence of being a radiant personality.
Even more, she gives evidence of Christian hope, for
no visit ever terminates but what, in some way, she gives

a testimony of her faith in Christ. The visitor leaves her bedside with the feeling that it was he who was most benefitted in the visit.

The benefit which the friendly visitor can bestow upon his visitee will be seen in the story about Mr. S.

Mr. S. is living in a rest home because he no longer is able to care for himself. He has lost his sight and, with the physical infirmity of his 86 years, needs the personal care which others can give him. But he is so lonely. He has no immediate family, just some kin living in another state. His real loneliness is that he cannot, because of his blindness, accommodate himself to his new and limited surroundings. The friendly visitor has meant much to him. He said, "I am so lonely. You don't know how much it means that you come and visit me." In the course of the conversation one day the friendly visitor learned that Mr. S. had had some training in reading by finger touch, but that it was an outmoded system. Inquiry revealed, however, that some material in that system was available. A subscription for it simply delighted Mr. S. And yet, what he enjoyed most was the visits, for he hungered for remembrance, attention, and the "give and take" of spirited conversation. The visitor will always remember his assurance: "You don't know what it means to me . . ."

Special Workers for

THE OLDER PERSON

A recurring wish of older people is to remain as efficient as possible as long as possible. The older member is helped to fulfill this wish when the congregation makes special effort to keep him in the worship and the life of the church, inaugurates fellowship or club programs in which he may participate, and extends to him a concerned hand through friendly visitors when he is a shut-in.

There comes a time, however, when additional and special services may be required to help the older member so that he can continue to live in his home and to enjoy living in the community where his family, friends, and fellow church members can be in touch with him. But the ability to stay in his home, where he has had so many pleasant and worthwhile experiences, may be seriously threatened by the onset of infirmity, disease, and handicap. When such a situation does develop, the congregation may add to its services by engaging special workers who will help the older member in his particular need or situation. For some of the simple tasks, volunteers may be secured; and for the more complex ones, paid workers may be engaged. Thus, special needs can be met by engaging such workers as:

A WEEKLY SHOPPER. Some older people are able to serve themselves in their homes but are unable to leave the premises to purchase the supplies they must have. They may depend on crutches, walkers, or wheel chairs to get about in the house, and by following certain self-developed methods, do quite well in maintaining themselves. But they are unable to leave the house, make their way over strange routes, or move about in crowded business places. A weekly shopper can secure a list of needs from the shut-in, make the purchases, and help him store the items in convenient places. A weekly shopper may thus enable the older member to remain in his own home instead of seeking institutional care.

A HOMEMAKER. A homemaker is a person who, through experience and maturity, is able to help an older person with the management of his home. Visiting on a regular schedule, perhaps weekly, the homemaker can give the house a cleaning, rub a tub of laundry, prepare a few dishes which can be stored in the refrigerator, change the bed linen, etc. Any one of these services, or a combination of them, can make it possible for an older member, when he is faced with such difficulties, to remain in his own home.

Some communities now provide professional homemakers. They work under the general supervision of a social worker or nurse. Such homemakers, chosen for their skills, are able to give a broader service by sharing their observations about the physical and emotional health of the older person with the supervisor of the homemaker program. Homemaker service is a community resource which the congregation can arrange for in the interest of older members needing such help.

A VISITING NURSE. The congregation may have within its membership trained nurses, who might be engaged to provide basic nursing care to older members. Extensive nursing care, of course, requires full duty, but a visiting nurse might be engaged by a congregation to serve older members who require injections, dressing of sores and infection, enemas, bathing, etc. Thus an older member could be helped by the congregation to remain in his own home, whereas, otherwise, he would require institutional care.

Many communities have Public Health Nursing services. Such services may go by different names in various localities, but they are administered by a public health nurse who has special training. Such service has the advantage that the nurse may be engaged on an hourly basis which would reduce cost and minimize the drain on the congregational budget. Most Public Health Nurses have had training to deal with chronic illness among older people. The congregation, in engaging such a worker, may find this community service to be the answer to a particular situation.

In planning for the welfare of the growing number of older people several neighboring congregations could cooperate in engaging the services of a visiting nurse and could, in this way, organize a mutual assistance program for older members.

A SOCIAL WORKER. Such a worker is a trained person skilled in dealing with people who have experienced difficulties which date from loss of social ties, loss of love, loss of contact with reality, lack of security, loneliness, or lack of social adjustment. Some congregations have added social workers to their staffs. A social worker can keep in touch with the aging and assess them and their ability to help themselves toward solutions of their problems. The social worker will be aware of situations where an older person needs specific help and will know what resources are available in the congregation and in the community.

A COORDINATOR OF FOSTER HOME SERVICES. Foster care has been practiced for many years as a service to children without a home or who, for some reason, could not remain in their own homes. The same service can be arranged for older people. The normal place for any person, of any age, is in his own home. When this becomes impossible the next best may be a home with a sustitute family. A good foster home can give a boarder most, if not all, the advantages of family life. The boarder pays for his service costs, but he is made to feel that he has a part in its activities.

A congregation may engage a person within its membership to discover what families would have the desire and facilities to open their homes to an older member and to include him in their family life. This worker will also determine what older members would be interested in such an arrangement. If the person so engaged is a social worker, or one who understands the implications of foster care, he will then endeavor to find the home where the foster family and the older member seeking care would be compatible, for the success of foster home care is based on: (a) The needs of the older person and the ability of the foster family to meet those needs. (b) The right of the older person to make suggestions about his living arrangements and the willingness of the foster family to "work out" these suggestions through mutual consideration. (c) The readiness of both parties to adapt themselves to changing conditions as time elapses. (d) The readiness of both parties to work closely with the coordinator, or his agent, to include any professional services which might be required, such as that of a doctor, nurse, social worker, and the like.

When the coordinator engaged by the congregation is not trained in social work principles he will make contact with a social work agency in the community and enlist services to match the older member and his needs with a foster family suited to supply his needs.

Another arrangement congregations may make is to have a social worker on the staff of the welfare agency which has been established among them who, among other duties, will be the resource person to work with the coordinator of the local congregation to develop the foster home program with its attendant services.

A DAY CENTER DIRECTOR. One way a congregation can serve older members is to provide a place in the church building for a day center. Here the older members can come at any time during the established hours of the day to read (library of books and magazines supplied by the congregation), play checkers, visit with a friend, chat with a group, work at a craft or hobby, and even be served a hot lunch. The last can be the answer for an older member who is alone during the day while other members of the household are busy at their places of employment. A day center can be an informal "get-together spot" for older people. When it is professionally supervised with planned activity the center can provide opportunity to make use of free time, to occupy empty and lonely hours, and to continue in ways which will help to keep the aging mentally and socially adjusted.

By engaging special workers, the congregation will assist older people to remain in their own homes beyond the time when, without such help, they would not be able to do so. In this way the congregation helps its aging members to remain happy, for a great source of happiness on the part of seniors is to remain in their homes as long as possible. Life at home contributes to their feelings of independence and comfort. However, the time will come for some when their best interests cannot be served in their own homes. Frequently this is the time when the older member needs counseling services so that he may be enabled to see his need clearly and also to determine how best to meet it.

When the time comes for an older member, because of infirmity, illness, or handicap, to leave his home, he will want to go to a place which is homelike; and the congregation can also have a part in providing such a place. This part is done by joining with other congregations to provide a church sponsored "home" for older people.

As was true in the past, so it is true now that there is a need for homes to care for the church's older members. Such homes are expensive to build and costly to operate—which emphasizes once again the sensible procedure on the part of the congregation to assist the older members to remain in their own homes as long as possible. But there will be those who must have care which goes beyond what can be supplied in the average private home. This need for congregate housing comes along with the further fact that older people are living longer and that some will outlive family members who could have given them assistance and care. Thus, to some seniors, a home for the aged serves as a symbol of the Good Samaritan. Moreover, when congregations work together to establish homes for the aged, they give a testimony to the church's concern for those members who, in their later years, need the love and concern of fellow Christians.

Bibliography

The body of material about the aged and aging has developed to sizable proportions and new works are added almost daily. This alone is an indication of the remarkable interest in this field. The following are intended to give the inquirer some reference material which will assist him in understanding and working with older people in the congregation and in the community.

BOOKS

Handbook of Aging and the Individual, edited by James E. Birren. The University of Chicago Press. $12.50. Extensive. Contributions from thirty scholars and scientists. Concerned with the biological and psychological bases for changes which occur in the aging individual's behavior and capacities.

Handbook of Social Gerontology, edited by Clark Tibbitts. The University of Chicago Press. $10.00. Extensive. Covers what is currently known about aging and deals with the effects of aging on the individual as a member of society and his impact on the values and institutions of society.

Understanding Old Age, by Jeanne G. Gilbert. The Ronald Press Co., New York. Basic information about normal and abnormal life changes in aging.

How to Help Older People, by Julietta K. Arthur. J. B. Lippincott Co., Philadelphia. Designed to help the family in planning for its older members especially with regard to living arrangements, financial aid, recreation, and health needs.

123

The Older People in Your Life, by Justus J. Schifferes. Pocket Books, Inc., New York. A 75-cent paperback. Written to help the lay person understand, help, enjoy, and get along better with older persons.

The Best Is Yet to Be, by Paul B. Maves. Westminster Press, Philadelphia. Experiences of later maturity with appropriate devotional resources.

The Church and the Older Person, by Robert M. Gray and David O. Moberg. William B. Eerdmans Publishing Co., Grand Rapids, Mich. Suggestions on ways the church can fulfill its obligations to its older members; also specifications indicating how seniors can be of help to the church.

New Church Programs with the Aging, by Elsie Culver. Association Press, New York. Defines problems of the older person in our society and outlines what the church can do about them.

Organized Religion and the Older Person, edited by D. Scudder. University of Florida Press, Gainesville. Series of conference papers in which religion is defined functionally and organizationally in relation to older people.

BOOKLETS

The Congregation and the Older Adult. Division of Welfare, National Lutheran Council, New York.

Older Persons in the Church Program. Board of Christian Education, Presbyterian Church in the U.S.A., Philadelphia.

Older Adults in the Church. The Methodist Publishing House, Nashville, Tenn. Guides which the congregation can use as a source for suggestions to serve the seniors in: worship, fellowship, recreation.

PAMPHLETS

Public Affairs Pamphlets 22 E. 38th Street, New York, offer:

No. 131 *When You Grow Older*

No. 139 *Live Long and Like It*

No. 174 *How to Be a Good Mother-in-law and Grandmother*

No. 182 *Getting Ready to Retire*

No. 196 *Mental Health—Everybody's Business*
No. 201 *Medical Research May Save Your Life*
No. 208 *When Parents Grow Old*
No. 276 *So You're Getting Older*
No. 347 *A Full Life after 65*

Developing Clubs for Older People, by Evelyn Brown Hoge. American Public Welfare Association, 1313 E. 60th St., Chicago. Also: *Helping Older Persons Remain in the Community, The Range of Public Welfare Services to Older People.*

Starting an Older Adult Group in Your Church. Department of Christian Education of Adults, P.O. Box 871, Nashville, Tenn. Also: *Older Adults in Christian Fellowship.*

PERIODICALS

Aging. U.S. Dept. of Health, Education and Welfare, Washington, D.C. Monthly publication which reports state programs on aging, conferences, latest publications.

Adding Life to Years, monthly bulletin published by State University of Iowa, Iowa City, Iowa. Reports on national developments on the planning of services to the aging. Each issue has a special bulletin carrying an extensive article on problems confronting seniors.

Mature Years, quarterly. Methodist Publishing Co., 810 Broadway, Nashville, Tenn. Has general and spiritual content for older persons.

Modern Maturity, by American Association of Retired Persons, Dupont Circle Bldg., 1346 Connecticut Ave. N.W., Washington 36, D.C. Comes every second month to those who pay membership fee of $2.00. Membership offers Insurance Plan, Drug Service and Travel Service.

Harvest Years, monthly from Harvest Years Circulation Dept., 680 Market St., San Francisco. $4.50. Valuable to those concerned about the social aspects of aging.

Geriatrics, monthly. Lancet Publications, Inc., 84 S. 10th St., Minneapolis. $6. Mainly technical medical aspects of aging but each issue carries excellent articles for the student and leader who works with seniors.

FILMS

Proud Years, 16mm, sound, 28 min. Yeshiva University, Audio-Visual Center, 526 W. 187th St., New York 33, N. Y. Rental $7. Details practical steps to help older people lead active, useful lives though handicapped. (Stroke in this instance.)

Aging: A Modern Achievement, 16mm, sound, 14 min. Dept. of Gerontology, University of Michigan, Ann Arbor. Rental $4.25. Guide $1. Uses charts that describe the social phenomenon of aging as an achievement of modern science and technology.

The Gift You Bring, 16 mm, 30 min. Portrays satisfactions of volunteers who worked in veterans hospitals. Free from local Veterans Administration Hospital.

Right at Home, 16mm, 28 min., rental $10.00. Deals with man and wife's problem—to live with a daughter or in a retirement home.

A Place to Live, 16mm, 25 min. National Council on Aging of the National Social Welfare Assembly, 345 E. 46th St., New York 25. Tensions and economic difficulties when an elderly man comes to live with married daughter. Solution looks at needs of seniors and how homes for the aged meet needs.

The Door That Opens Wide, 16mm, 27 min. Hartford, Conn., Council of Churches, Social Service Dept., 315 Pearl St., Hartford. Foster homes for seniors with appropriate pastoral and case work help.

PLAYS

A Choice to Make, by Nora Sterling. Division of Family Service Association of America, 44 E. 23rd Street, New York 10. Review copy is available at $2.00. Shows that each of us has the privilege of accepting or rejecting the life we want to live in the later years. The main character is helped to see that unhappiness is often self-inflicted. Also available: *Ever Since April,* on problems of retirement.

The Room Upstairs, production packet for $5. Good for discussion on problems of the old and young living together. Human Relations Aids, Room 713, 1790 Broadway, New York 19.

It Isn't Always Easy, by Merrill Rogers. University of Michigan Press, Ann Arbor, Mich. $1 per copy. Production packet, with 6 copies, includes directions for the play and summary discussion at $5. Help to train volunteers to work with the aged.

SERVING THE HOMEBOUND

Chronic Illness Newsletter, monthly. American Medical Association, 535 N. Dearborn, Chicago. Free.

Homemaker Service Bulletin, monthly. American Medical Association, 535 N. Dearborn St., Chicago, Ill. 60610. Free.

Comfort and Strength. Inspirational, thoughtful leaflets for the ill and troubled. 1720 Chouteau St., St. Louis, Mo. Catalogue available.

The Mature Heart, by Helen B. Emmons. Abingdon Press, Nashville, Tenn. Devotional material in large print. $3.50.

Comfort Ye My People, by Russell Dicks. Macmillan Co., New York. $1.50. Religious resources helpful in a ministry to the ill.

Ye Visited Me, by Harold W. Reisch. Board of Social Missions, Lutheran Church in America, 231 Madison Ave., New York 16. 20 cents.

Portals of Prayer and *Upper Room.* Well-known devotional booklets, suggested because they have large print.

Fast Falls the Eventide, by Olle Nystedt. Augsburg Publishing House, 426 S. Fifth St., Minneapolis, Minn. 55415. $2.00.

At Eventide, by Gootfrid Billing. Augsburg Publishing House, 426 S. Fifth St., Minneapolis, Minn. 55415. $1.50

The Christian Magnifier. 8-page monthly (except summer). $1 per year. The Lutheran Braille Evangelism Association, 104 W. Franklin, Minneapolis 3. Large print of spiritual content.

Homemaker Services for Older People. Office of Aging, Welfare Administration, U.S. Dept. of Health, Education and Welfare. Selected references No. 2, Washington, D.C. Free.

Guide for Developing a Friendly Visiting Program. California Department of Social Welfare "References," Sacramento.

A Friendly Visiting Program, No. 13. 15 cents. Government Printing Office, Washington 25, D.C.

The Author

In writing this book about the aging and their needs, the Rev. Arthur P. Rismiller has drawn on a wide range of experience in working with older people. This background includes parish work, pastoral clinical training, participation in institutes on aging, and chaplaincy services among institutionalized older people.

Pastor Rismiller has, since 1955, served as geriatrics chaplain for the Lutheran Welfare League, Columbus, Ohio. Previous to his present position, he was a parish minister for more than 20 years.

He has served as staff coordinator for the Lutheran Welfare League in the sponsorship and construction of Lutheran Senior City, a retirement center for older people in Columbus; as the originator and director of a church-adopt-a-rest-home plan among such facilities in that city; and as a community resource person in the training of volunteers for visiting services among aged shut-ins.

Pastor Rismiller has written several articles for periodicals on problems of the aging and has participated in the work of church and civic groups dealing with such problems. He is a graduate of Capital University and the Evangelical Lutheran Theological Seminary, Columbus.